Fre

MW01075759

Texas
FIELD GUIDE

by Dan Johnson

Adventure Publications, Inc.
Cambridge, MN

DEDICATION

To my children, Jacob, Joshua and Emily, and wife, Julie, with all my heart; to the parents who encouraged my interest in nature and writing; and to our Father in Heaven for this glorious creation and the loved ones with whom we share its wonders.

ACKNOWLEDGEMENTS

Special thanks to the Texas Parks and Wildlife Department, the U.S. Fish and Wildlife Service, Dr. Hal Schramm of Mississippi State University, and everyone at Adventure Publications.

Edited by Brett Ortler

Cover and book design by Jonathan Norberg

Illustration credits by artist and page number:

Cover illustrations: Guadalupe Bass (main) by Joseph Tomelleri; Bluegill (upper front cover and back cover) by Duane Raver/USFWS

Timothy Knepp/USFWS: 118 **Julie Martinez:** 62 (main), 64 (left and middle insets), 96 (right inset), 100 (insets), 106 (right inset), 120 (both) **MyFWC.com/fishing:** 12 **Duane Raver/USFWS:** 10 (both), 18, 24, 26, 28, 30, 32 (main), 34, 42, 44, 46, 48, 52, 64 (main), 66, 68 (main), 102, 112, 124, 130, 132, 138, 146, 148, 152, 154, 156, 158, 162, 164, 166, 170, 172, 174, 176 **Joseph Tomelleri:** 32 (inset), 36 (both), 38, 40 (both), 54, 56, 58, 60 (both), 62 (Sailfin Molly inset), 64 (right inset), 68 (insets), 70, 72 (both), 74, 76, 78, 80 (both), 82 (both), 84 (both), 86, 90, 92, 94, 96 (main, left inset), 98 (both), 100 (main), 104 (both), 106 (main, left inset), 108, 110, 114, 116, 122, 126 (both), 128, 134, 136, 140, 142, 144, 150, 160 (main, Dollar Sunfish inset), 168, 178

Copyright 2009 by Dan Johnson
Published by Adventure Publications, Inc.
820 Cleveland St. S
Cambridge, MN 55008
1-800-678-7006
www.adventurepublications.net
Printed in China
ISBN-13: 978-1-59193-216-1
ISBN-10: 1-59193-216-5

TABLE OF CONTENTS

Bowfin Family

Catfish Family

4

HOW TO USE THIS BOOK

Your *Freshwater Fish of Texas Field Guide* is designed to make it easy to identify 78 of the most common and important species in Texas, and learn fascinating facts about each one's range, natural history and more.

The fish are organized by families, such as Catfish (*Ictaluridae*), Perch (*Percidae*), Trout and Salmon (*Salmonidae*) and Sunfish (*Centrarchidae*), which are listed in alphabetical order. Within these families, individual species are arranged alphabetically in their appropriate groups. For example, members of the Sunfish family are divided into the Black Bass, Crappie and True Sunfish groups. For a detailed list of fish families and individual species, turn to the Table of Contents (page 3); the Index (pp. 186-191) provides a handy reference guide to fish by common name (such as Rainbow Trout) and other common terms for the species.

Fish Identification

Determining a fish's body shape is the first step to identifying it. Each fish family usually exhibits one or sometimes two basic outlines. Catfish have long, stout bodies with flattened heads, barbels or "whiskers" around the mouth, a relatively tall but narrow dorsal fin and an adipose fin. There are two forms of Sunfish: the flat, round, plate-like outline we see in Bluegills; and the torpedo or "fusiform" shape of Largemouth Bass.

In this field guide you can quickly identify a fish by first matching its general body shape to one of the fish family silhouettes listed in the Table of Contents. From there, turn to that family's section and use the illustrations and text descriptions to identify your fish. A Sample Page (pg. 22) is provided to explain how the information is presented in each two-page spread.

For some species, the illustration will be enough to identify your catch, but it is important to note that your fish may not look exactly like the artwork. Fish frequently change colors. Males that are brightly colored during the spawning season may show muted coloration at other times. Likewise, bass caught in muddy streams show much less pattern than those taken from clear lakes—and all fish lose some of their markings and color when removed from the water.

Most fish are similar in appearance to one or more other species—often, but not always, within the same family. For example, the Black Crappie is remarkably similar to the White Crappie. To accurately identify such look-alikes, check the inset illustrations and accompanying notes below the main illustration, under the "Similar Species" heading.

Throughout *Fish of Texas* we use basic biological and fisheries management terms that refer to physical characteristics or conditions of fish and their environment, such as "*dorsal*" fin or "*turbid*" water. For your convenience, these are listed and defined in the Glossary (pp. 180-185), along with other handy fish-related terms and their definitions.

Understanding such terminology will help you make sense of reports on state and federal research, fish population surveys, lake assessments, management plans and other important fisheries documents.

FISH ANATOMY

It's much easier to identify fish if you know the names of different parts of a fish. For example, it's easier to use the term "adipose" fin to indicate the small, soft, fleshy flap on an Rainbow Trout's back than to try to describe it. The following illustrations point out the basic parts of a fish; the accompanying text defines these characteristics.

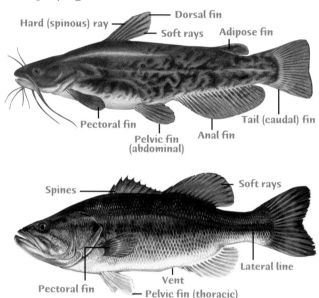

Fins are made up of bony structures that support a membrane. There are three kinds of bony structures in fins: **Soft rays** are flexible fin supports and are often branched.

Spines are stiff, often sharp, supports that are not jointed. **Hard rays** are stiff, pointed, barbed structures that can be raised or lowered. Catfish are famous for their hard rays, which are often mistakenly called spines. Sunfish have soft rays associated with spines to form a prominent dorsal fin.

Fins are named by their position on the fish. The **dorsal fin** is on top along the midline. A few species have another fin on their back, called an **adipose fin**. This small, fleshy protuberance located between the dorsal fin and the tail is distinctive of catfish, trout and salmon. **Pectoral fins** are found on each side of the fish near the gills. The **anal fin** is located along the midline, on the fish's bottom, or *ventral,* side. There is also a paired set of fins on the bottom of the fish, called the **pelvic fins**. These can be in the **thoracic position** (just below the pectoral fins) or farther back on the stomach, in the **abdominal position**. The tail is known as the **caudal fin**.

Eyes—A fish's eyes can detect color. Their eyes are rounder than those of mammals because of the refractive index of water; focus is achieved by moving the lens in and out, not distorting it as in mammals. Different species have varying levels of eyesight. Walleyes see well in low light. Bluegills have excellent daytime vision but see poorly at night, making them vulnerable to predation.

Nostrils—A pair of nostrils, or *nares*, is used to detect odors in the water. Eels and catfishes have particularly well-developed senses of smell.

Mouth—The shape of the mouth is a clue to what the fish eats. The larger the food it consumes, the larger the mouth.

Teeth—Not all fish have teeth, but those that do have mouth gear designed to help them feed. Walleyes, Northern Pike and Chain Pickerel have sharp *canine* teeth for grabbing and holding prey. Minnows have *pharyngeal* teeth—located in the throat—for grinding.

Catfish have *cardiform* teeth, which feel like a rough patch in the front of the mouth. Bass have patches of *vomerine* teeth on the roofs of their mouths.

Swim Bladder—Almost all fish have a swim bladder, a balloon-like organ that helps the fish regulate its buoyancy.

Lateral Line—This sensory organ helps the fish detect movement in the water (to help avoid predators or capture prey) as well as water currents and pressure changes. It consists of fluid-filled sacs with hair-like sensors, which are open to the water through a row of pores in their skin along each side—creating a visible line along the fish's side.

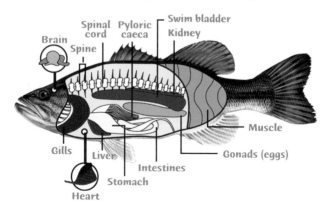

FISH NAMES

A Walleye is a Walleye in Texas. But in the northern parts of its range, Canadians call it a jack or jackfish. In the eastern U.S., it is often called a pickerel or walleyed pike.

Because common names may vary regionally, and even change for different sizes of the same species, scientific names are used that are exactly the same around the world. Each species has only one correct scientific name that can be recognized anywhere, in any language. The Walleye is *Sander vitreus* from Dallas to Dublin.

Scientific names are made up of Greek or Latin words that often describe the species. There are two parts to a scientific name: the generic or "genus," which is capitalized (*Sander*), and the specific name, which is not capitalized (*vitreus*). Both are displayed in italic text.

A species' genus represents a group of closely related fish. The Walleye and Sauger are in the same genus, so they share the generic name *Sander*. But each have different specific names, *vitreus* for Walleye, *canadense* for the Sauger.

ABOUT TEXAS FISH

Texas is blessed with rich aquatic diversity. Habitats range from Plains streams and isolated springs to sprawling impoundments. As a result, Texas offers a variety of opportunities to watch, study and pursue fish. This guide covers the species most commonly enjoyed by anglers, along with a variety of native and introduced species.

FREQUENTLY ASKED QUESTIONS

What is a fish?

Fish are aquatic, typically cold-blooded animals that have backbones, gills and fins.

Are all fish cold-blooded?

All freshwater fish are cold-blooded. Recently it has been discovered that some members of the saltwater Tuna family are warm-blooded. Whales and Bottlenose Dolphins are also warm-blooded, but they are mammals, not fish.

Do all fish have scales?

No. Most fish have scales that look like those on the Common Goldfish. A few, such as Alligator Gar, have scales that resemble armor plates. Catfish have no scales at all.

How do fish breathe?

A fish takes in water through its mouth and forces it through its gills, where a system of fine membranes absorbs oxygen from the water, and releases carbon dioxide. Gills cannot pump air efficiently over these membranes, which quickly dry out and stick together. Fish should never be out of the water longer than you can hold your breath.

Can fish breathe air?

Some species can; gars have a modified swim bladder that acts like a lung. Fish that can't breathe air may die when dissolved oxygen in the water falls below critical levels.

How do fish swim?

Fish swim by contracting bands of muscles on alternate sides of their body so the tail is whipped rapidly from side to side. Pectoral and pelvic fins are used mainly for stability when a fish hovers, but are sometimes used during rapid bursts of forward motion.

Do all fish look like fish?

Most do and are easily recognizable as fish. The eels and lampreys are fish, but they look like snakes. Alligator Gar look like prehistoric monsters, but of course they aren't.

Where can you find fish?

Some fish species can be found in almost any body of water, but not all fish are found everywhere. Each is designed to exploit a particular habitat. The Mexican Stoneroller is found in riffles and runs of small pools, while the Blue Catfish prefers large rivers and reservoirs.

A species may move around within its home water, sometimes migrating hundreds of miles between lakes, rivers and tributary streams. Some movements, such as spawning migrations, are seasonal and very predictable.

Fish may also move horizontally from one area to another or vertically in the water column in response to changes in environmental conditions and food availability. In addition, many fish have daily travel patterns. By studying a species' habitat, food and spawning information in this book—and understanding how it interacts with other Texas fish—it is possible to make an educated prediction of where to find it in any lake, stream or river.

INVASIVE SPECIES

While many introduced species have great recreational value, such as Largemouth Bass, many exotic species have caused problems. Never move fish, water or vegetation from one lake or stream to another. For details, visit the Parks and Wildlife Department's website, www.tpwd.state.tx.us.

FUN WITH FISH

There are many ways to enjoy Texas' fish, from reading about them in this book to watching them in the wild. You can don a dive mask and jump in, wear polarized glasses to observe them from above the surface, or use an underwater camera (or sonar) to monitor fish behavior year-round.

Hands-on activities are also popular. Some 2.4 million residents and nonresidents enjoy fishing in Texas each year. The sport provides a great chance to spend time with family and friends and, in many cases, bring home a healthy meal of fresh fish.

Proceeds from license sales, along with special federal excise taxes on fishing gear and motorboat fuel, help the Texas Parks and Wildlife Department's Inland Fisheries Division manage, protect and enhance precious aquatic resources. The sport also has a $2 billion impact on the state's economy, supporting thousands of jobs in fishing, tourism and related industries.

OPPORTUNITIES FOR NONRESIDENTS

More than 220,000 nonresidents sample the remarkable fishing in Texas each year. A wealth of resources are available to help out-of-state anglers (as well as Texans) enjoy the full bounty of opportunities. One excellent source is the Texas Parks and Wildlife Department's website, www. tpwd.state.tx.us. You may also contact the department's main office in Austin at (800) 792-1112. In addition, guides, tackle shops and bait dealers are great resources to exploring the Lone Star State. Finally, the Texas Freshwater Fisheries Center in Athens, (903) 676-2277, is a wonderful place for residents and nonresidents alike to learn more about the state's fish.

CATCH-AND-RELEASE FISHING

Selective harvest (keeping some fish to eat and releasing the rest) and total catch-and-release fishing allow anglers to enjoy the sport without harming the resource. Catch-and-release is especially important with certain species and sizes of fish, and in lakes or rivers where biologists are trying to improve the fishery by protecting large predators or breeding age, adult fish. The fishing regulations, Parks and Wildlife website and your local fisheries office are excellent sources of advice on which fish to keep or release.

Catch-and-release is only truly successful if the fish survives the experience. Following are helpful tips to help reduce the chances of post-release mortality.

- Play and land fish quickly.

- Wet your hands before touching a fish, to avoid removing its protective slime coating.

- Handle the fish gently and keep it in the water if possible.

- Do not hold the fish by the eye sockets or gills; hold it horizontally and support its belly.

- If a fish is deeply hooked, cut the line so at least an inch hangs outside the mouth. This helps the hook lie flush when the fish takes in food.

- Circle hooks may help reduce deeply hooked fish.

- Don't fish deep water unless you plan to keep your catch.

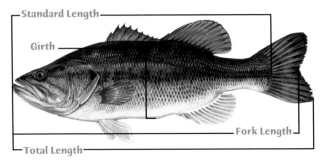

FISH MEASUREMENT

Fish are measured in three ways: standard length, fork length and total length. The first two are more accurate, because tails are often damaged or worn down. Total length is used in slot limits.

The following formulas estimate the weight of popular game fish. Lengths are in inches; weights are in pounds.

Formulas

Bass weight = (length x length x girth) / 1,200
Pike weight = (length x length x length) / 3,500
Sunfish weight = (length x length x length) / 1,200
Trout weight = (length x girth x girth) / 800
Walleye weight = (length x length x length) / 2,700

For example, let's say that you catch a 16-inch Walleye. Using the formula for Walleyes above: (16 x 16 x 16) divided by 2,700 = 1.5 pounds. Your Walleye would weigh approximately 1.5 pounds.

FISH CONSUMPTION ADVISORIES

Most fish are safe for us to eat. They are also a healthy source of low-fat protein. But because most of the world's surface water contains some industrial pollutants, any store-bought or sport-caught fish could contain contaminants.

The Texas Department of State Health Services (TDSHS) monitors fish in the state for the presence of environmental contaminants and alerts the public through bans (closures) and advisories when a threat to human health may occur from the consumption of contaminated fish. For more information, visit www.dshs.state.tx.us/seafood/ or call the TDSHS at (512) 834-6757.

TEXAS STATE RECORD FISH

SPECIES	WEIGHT (LBS.)	WHERE CAUGHT	YEAR
Bass, Guadalupe	3.69	Travis	1983
Bass, Guadalupe X Smallmouth	4.69	San Marcos River	1999
Bass, Guadalupe X Spotted	3.06	Lady Bird Lake	2007
Bass, Largemouth	18.18	Lake Fork	1992
Bass, Palmetto	19.66	Ray Hubbard	1984
Bass, Rock	0.90	San Marcos River	2002
Bass, Smallmouth	7.93	Meredith	1998
Bass, Spotted	5.56	Lake O' the Pines	1966
Bass, Striped	53.00	Brazos River	1999
Bass, White	5.56	Colorado River	1977
Bass, White X Yellow	4.75	Lake Fork	2005
Bass, Yellow	2.38	Sabine River	2006
Bluegill	2.02	Lampasas River	1999
Bowfin	17.65	Lake Fork	1993
Buffalo, Bigmouth	58.75	Sam Rayburn	1994
Buffalo, Black	34.88	Texoma	2004
Bullhead, Black	5.15	Brazos River	2007
Bullhead, Yellow	3.20	Lake Fork	1997
Carp, Bighead	90.00	Kirby	2000
Carp, Common	43.13	Lady Bird Lake	2006
Carp, Grass	53.50	Toledo River	2006
Carpsucker, River	2.10	Trinity River	1996
Catfish, Blue	121.50	Texoma	2004
Catfish, Channel	36.50	Pedernales River	1965
Catfish, Flathead	98.50	Palestine	1998
Catfish Retail	1.48	Cal Young Park Lake	2002
Catfish, Suckermouth	1.75	Calaveras	2006
Cichlid, Rio Grande	1.59	Llano River	2001
Corvina, Orangemouth	16.31	Calaveras	1991
Crappie, Black	3.92	Lake Fork	2003
Crappie, White	4.56	Navarro Mills	1968
Drum, Black	4.25	Calaveras	2006
Drum, Freshwater	34.70	Texoma	1995
Drum, Red	36.83	Fairfield	2001
Eel, American	6.45	Lady Bird Lake	2001
Flounder, Southern	11.35	Brazoria Reservoir	1987
Gar, Alligator	279.00	Rio Grande	1951
Gar, Longnose	50.31	Trinity River	1954
Gar, Shortnose	3.90	Arrowhead	1995
Gar, Spotted	9.80	Mexia	1994
Goldeye	2.31	Texoma	1996

SPECIES	WEIGHT (LBS.)	WHERE CAUGHT	YEAR
Herring, Skipjack	0.30	Trinity River	2003
Killifish, Gulf	0.02	Twin Buttes	2006
Ladyfish	0.24	Trinity River	2000
Logperch	0.01	Stillhouse Hollow	2002
Minnow, Bullhead	0.01	Whitney	1996
Mosquitofish	2.48 inches	Canton City	2007
Mullet, White	1.16	Brays Bayou	1998
Needlefish, Atlantic	0.15	Trinity River	2005
Oscar	1.21	Greenbelt	1998
Pacu, Red-bellied	8.95	San Marcos River	2006
Perch, Nile	12.06	Victor Braunig	1980
Perch, Yellow	1.04	Meredith	1996
Pickerel, Chain	4.75	Pat Mayse	1996
Pickerel, Redfin	0.44	Sam Rayburn	1995
Pike, Northern	18.28	Lady Bird Lake	1981
Redhorse, Gray	1.18	Medina River	2005
Saugeye	7.78	Kirby	1998
Seatrout, Spotted X Corvina	20.80	Victor Braunig	1192
Shad, Gizzard	2.67	Lady Bird Lake	1997
Shad, Threadfin	0.13	Richland-Chambers	1998
Shiner, Blacktail	0.05	Attoyac River	2006
Shiner, Golden	0.52	Placid	1996
Silverside, Inland	0.02	Benbrook	1994
Sleeper, Bigmouth	2.42	Nueces River	2005
Sucker, Spotted	1.41	Catfish Creek	2002
Sunfish, Green	1.30	Burke-Crenshaw Lake	2005
Sunfish, Hybrid Green	0.30	Belton	2006
Sunfish, Longear	0.48	Lake Fork	1998
Sunfish, Orangespotted	0.18	Lake Fork	2005
Sunfish, Other Hybrid	1.73	Bardwell	2004
Sunfish, Redbreast	1.63	Comal River	1997
Sunfish, Redear	2.99	Lady Bird Lake	1997
Sunfish, Spotted	0.12	Onion Creek	1993
Tarpon	10.12	Victor Braunig	1986
Tiger Muskellunge	9.06	Nocona	1979
Tilapia, Blue	6.25	Gibbons Creek Reservoir	1995
Tilapia, Hybrid	3.75	Gibbons Creek Reservoir	1993
Topminnow, Blackstripe	0.02	Lower Waterworks	2002
Trout, Brook	0.67	Guadalupe River	1984
Trout, Brown	7.12	Guadalupe River	1986
Trout, Rainbow	8.24	Guadalupe River	2001
Walleye	11.88	Meredith	1990
Warmouth	1.30	Lady Bird Lake	1991

These pages explain how the information is presented for each fish.

SAMPLE FISH ILLUSTRATION

Description: brief summary of physical characteristics to help you identify the fish, such as coloration and markings, body shape, fin size and placement

Similar Species: lists other fish that look similar and the pages on which they can be found; also includes detailed inset drawings (below) highlighting physical traits such as markings, mouth size or shape and fin characteristics to help you distinguish this fish from similar species

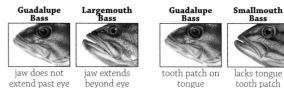

Guadalupe Bass	Largemouth Bass	Guadalupe Bass	Smallmouth Bass
jaw does not extend past eye	jaw extends beyond eye	tooth patch on tongue	lacks tongue tooth patch

SAMPLE COMPARE ILLUSTRATIONS

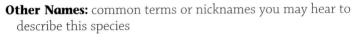

COMMON NAME
Scientific Name

Other Names: common terms or nicknames you may hear to describe this species

Habitat: environment where the fish is found (such as streams, rivers, small or large lakes, fast-flowing or still water, in or around vegetation, near shore, in clear water)

Range: geographic distribution, starting with the fish's overall range, followed by state-specific information

Food: what the fish eats most of the time (such as crustaceans, insects, fish, plankton)

Reproduction: timing of and behavior during the spawning period (dates and water temperatures, migration information, preferred spawning habitat, type of nest if applicable, colonial or solitary nester, parental care for eggs or fry)

Average Size: average length or range of length, average weight or range of weight

Records: state—the state record for this species, location and year; North American—the North American record for this species, location and year (based on the Fresh Water Fishing Hall of Fame)

Notes: Interesting natural history information. This can include unique behaviors, remarkable features, sporting and table quality, details on migrations, seasonal patterns or population trends

Description: mottled olive green back fading to light green sides and whitish belly; long cylindrical body; forward-facing mouth; long, dark green dorsal fin

Similar Species: American Eel (pg. 44), Northern Snakehead

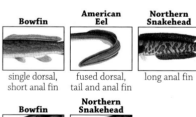

Bowfin	American Eel	Northern Snakehead
single dorsal, short anal fin	fused dorsal, tail and anal fin	long anal fin

Bowfin	Northern Snakehead
lacks scales on head	large scales on head

BOWFIN

Amia calva

Other Names: cypress trout, dogfish, grindle, grinnel, mudfish

Habitat: clear, weedy areas of warmwater lakes; pools and backwaters of rivers and streams

Range: native to the eastern U.S. from the Mississippi River to the St. Lawrence drainage south to Texas and Florida; in Texas, the Red, Sabine and San Jacinto drainages and downstream sections of the Brazos and Colorado rivers

Food: fish, crayfish, frogs and other aquatic animals

Reproduction: when water temperature surpasses 60 degrees, male builds circular nest; female lays up to 64,000 eggs that hatch in 8-10 days; male guards eggs and fry

Average Size: 23 to 27 inches, 6 to 8 pounds

Records: State—17 pounds, 10 ounces, Lake Fork, 1993; North American—21 pounds, 8 ounces, Forest Lake, South Carolina, 1980

Notes: Bowfins are voracious predators that hold in deep water by day and venture into shallows at night to feed. An air breather, Bowfins can survive extreme oxygen depletion. Live specimens have been found buried deep in the mud beneath dried ponds. Once considered a threat to game fish, it is now considered beneficial as it controls rough fish. Not widely sought by anglers, but puts up a good fight. Similar to the non-native Northern Snakehead, which biologists fear could invade state waters.

Description: back black to olive; sides yellowish-green; belly cream to yellow; light bar on base of tail; barbels (dark at base) around mouth; adipose fin; scaleless skin; rounded tail

Similar Species: Flathead Catfish (pg. 34), Yellow Bullhead (pg. 28)

Black Bullhead	Yellow Bullhead		Black Bullhead	Flathead Catfish
usually 17 to 21 anal fin rays	usually 24 to 27 anal fin rays		slight overbite	pronounced underbite

Black Bullhead	Yellow Bullhead
olive back and sides	yellowish back and sides

26

BLACK BULLHEAD
Ameiurus melas

Ictaluridae

Other Names: common bullhead, horned pout, mud cat, polliwog

Habitat: shallow, slow-moving streams and backwaters; lakes and ponds; tolerates extremely turbid (cloudy) conditions

Range: southern Canada through the Great Lakes and the Mississippi River watershed into the Southwest; statewide in Texas, except the Trans-Pecos drainage

Food: a scavenging opportunist, feeds mostly on animal material (live or dead) but will eat plant matter

Reproduction: spawns in spring into early summer; excavates nest in shallow water; both sexes guard nest and eggs, which hatch in 4 to 6 days; fry school in tight swarms along shorelines through their first summer

Average Size: 6 to 10 inches; 4 ounces to 1 pound

Records: State—5 pounds, 2 ounces, Brazos River, 2007; North American—8 pounds, 15 ounces, Sturgis Pond, Michigan, 1987

Notes: A native species, the Black Bullhead is sometimes considered a pest due to its small size and because it competes with more desirable fish. Still, it is easy to catch and its white fillets have a good flavor, though the meat can become soft. It tolerates silt, pollution, low oxygen levels and tepid water better than most fish. Adults typically rest in deep water during the day, and move into the shallows to scavenge at night.

Description: olive head and back; yellowish-green sides; white belly; barbels on lower jaw are pale green to white; scaleless skin; adipose fin; rounded tail

Similar Species: Black Bullhead (pg. 26), Flathead Catfish (pg. 34)

Yellow Bullhead	Black Bullhead	Yellow Bullhead	Flathead Catfish
usually 24 to 27 anal fin rays	usually 17 to 21 anal fin rays	slight overbite	pronounced underbite

Yellow Bullhead	Black Bullhead
yellowish back and sides	olive back and sides

28

YELLOW BULLHEAD

Ameiurus natalis

Other Names: white-whiskered bullhead, yellow cat

Habitat: medium-sized streams and shallows of warmwater lakes; prefers clear water and rocky bottom

Range: southern Great Lakes through the eastern U.S. to the Gulf and into Mexico, introduced in the West; widespread in Texas, excluding the Panhandle and Trans-Pecos drainages

Food: a scavenging opportunist that feeds mainly at night on aquatic insects, crayfish, snails, small fish and plant matter

Reproduction: in early summer, male and female build nest in shallow water, typically on sand or rocky bottom that is shaded by cover; between 2,000 to 12,000 eggs are produced; both parents guard eggs and young

Average Size: 7 to 13 inches, 4 to 19 ounces

Records: State—3 pounds, 3 ounces, Lake Fork, 1997; North American—4 pounds, 15 ounces, Ogeechie River, Georgia, 2003

Notes: Uses its acute sense of smell to locate food and in social behavior. Although it is found in streams with permanent flow, it tends to avoid strong currents. Not widely pursued by anglers, but its cream-colored flesh has an excellent flavor, though it may become soft in the summer months. Easiest to catch when fishing at night and using worms or crickets. More carnivorous than the Black Bullhead.

Description: pale bluish-silver to slate gray back and sides (similar to channel catfish but lacks spots on back and sides); light underside; forked tail

Similar Species: Channel Catfish (pg. 32)

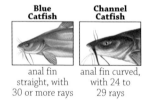

Blue Catfish	Channel Catfish
anal fin straight, with 30 or more rays	anal fin curved, with 24 to 29 rays

BLUE CATFISH

Ictalurus furcatus

Other Names: blue fulton, chucklehead, silver or white cat

Habitat: large rivers and reservoirs; prefers strong current and silt-free bottom such as sand, gravel or small rocks

Range: native to the Mississippi River basin and Gulf Slope drainages from Minnesota south to Alabama and New Mexico; found across much of Texas, including the Panhandle, but not in the northwest

Food: fish, insects, crayfish, mussels

Reproduction: matures at about 24 inches in length; spawns April through June when water temperatures reach 70 to 75 degrees; male fans out nest in a cavity such as a hole in the bank; female deposits an egg mass; male guards eggs

Average Size: 20 to 44 inches, 3 to 40 pounds

Records: State—121 pounds, 8 ounces, Lake Texoma, 2004; North American—124 pounds, Mississippi River, Illinois, 2005

Notes: Thanks to its large size, fighting power and fine flavor, the Blue Catfish is a favorite of anglers. Fifty-pound fish are not uncommon in healthy fisheries and giant Blue Catfish weighing more than 300 pounds were reported prior to 1900. It is a big-water species found in the main channels and major tributaries of large rivers, as well as reservoirs. At times, it migrates in response to water temperature; its preferred range is 77 to 82 degrees.

31

CHANNEL CATFISH

HEADWATER CATFISH

Description: gray to silver back and sides; white belly; black spots on sides; large fish lack spots and are olive or slate; forked tail; adipose fin; long barbels around mouth

Similar Species: Blue Catfish (pg. 30), Bullheads (pp. 26-29), Flathead Catfish (pg. 34), Headwater Catfish

Channel Catfish	Flathead Catfish	Bullheads	Headwater Catfish
forked tail	squared tail	tail rounded or slightly notched	tail moderately forked

Channel Catfish	Blue Catfish
anal fin curved 24-29 rays	anal fin straight 30 or more rays

32

CHANNEL CATFISH

Ictalurus punctatus

Other Names: spotted, speckled or silver catfish, fiddler

Habitat: prefers clean streams with moderate current, deep pools and sand, gravel or rubble bottom; stocked in many lakes; can tolerate turbid (cloudy) backwaters

Range: southern Canada through the Midwest into Mexico, introduced through much of the U.S.; statewide in Texas

Food: insects, crustaceans, fish, some plant matter

Reproduction: matures at 3 to 6 years; spawns when water is 70 to 85 degrees; male builds a nest in a sheltered area; female lays 2,000-21,000 eggs; male guards eggs and young

Average Size: 12 to 20 inches, 3 to 4 pounds

Records: State—36 pounds, 8 ounces, Pedernales River, 1965; North American—58 pounds, Santee Cooper Reservoir, South Carolina, 1964

Notes: The third most popular freshwater sport fish in Texas, the Channel Catfish is a strong fighter and can be caught on a variety of prepared baits ranging from doughballs to stinkbaits. Its white, sweet-tasting fillets are excellent table fare. Often remains in deep water during the day, then moves into shallow feeding areas at night. Uses taste buds in its barbels and skin to locate food, but its large eyes also allow sight-feeding. Usually a bottom feeder, it suspends or rises to the surface on occasion. Similar in appearance to the Headwater Catfish found in the Pecos and Rio Grande drainages.

Description: color variable, usually mottled yellow or brown; belly cream to yellow; adipose fin; chin barbels; lacks scales; head broad and flat; tail squared; pronounced underbite

Similar Species: Bullheads (pp. 26-28), Channel Catfish (pg. 32)

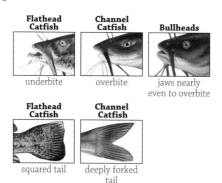

Flathead Catfish	Channel Catfish	Bullheads
underbite	overbite	jaws nearly even to overbite

Flathead Catfish	Channel Catfish
squared tail	deeply forked tail

FLATHEAD CATFISH

Pylodictis olivaris

Other Names: shovelnose, shovelhead, yellow cat, mud cat, pied cat, Mississippi cat

Habitat: deep pools of large rivers and impoundments; often found near cover and in fast water below dams

Range: the Mississippi River watershed and into Mexico, large rivers in the Southwest; statewide in Texas

Food: fish, crayfish

Reproduction: spawns in spring and early summer when water is 72 to 80 degrees; male builds and defends nest in hollow log, undercut bank or another secluded area; female may lay more than 60,000 eggs, depending on her size and condition; male guards young for 7 days after hatching

Average Size: 15 to 45 inches; 1 to 45 pounds

Records: State—98 pounds, 8 ounces, Lake Palestine, 1998; North American—123 pounds, Elk River Reservoir, Kansas, 1998

Notes: Feeds aggressively on live fish, often at night, when it moves from deep water to riffles and shallow areas. Unlike the Channel Catfish, it is not a scavenger and rarely eats decaying animal matter. Has been introduced into some lakes to control stunted panfish and bullhead populations; it is a species of concern in some non-native areas where it is blamed for reducing native fish populations. A strong fighter with firm, white flesh.

TADPOLE MADTOM

FRECKLED MADTOM

Description: dark olive to brown back and sides, fading to whitish belly; dark line on side; large, fleshy head; barbels around mouth

Similar Species: Bullheads (pp. 26-29), Freckled Madtom

Tadpole Madtom	Bullheads	Tadpole Madtom	Freckled Madtom
fused adipose fin	free adipose fin	jaws even	pronounced overbite

TADPOLE MADTOM

Noturus gyrinus

Other Names: willow cat

Habitat: lakes, ponds, sloughs, streams and large rivers; prefers moderate to slack current areas with soft or rocky bottom and ample weed growth

Range: widespread in much of the eastern U.S. except the Appalachians; found in central and eastern Texas from the Red River to the Nueces basin

Food: insects, crustaceans, plant matter, fish

Reproduction: spawns in late spring to early summer; eggs are deposited in the nest located under stones, roots, or in abandoned crayfish burrows; one or both parents (usually the male) defends nest and cares for the eggs

Average Size: up to 4 inches

Records: none

Notes: A small, secretive member of the catfish family, the Tadpole Madtom spends the day hiding in heavy cover and is most active at night. Though small, it is well armed. Poison glands at the base of the dorsal and pectoral fins, coupled with special sheaths on the spines of these fins, are capable of delivering a painful "sting." Used as baitfish in some areas of the country. Similar in appearance to the Freckled Madtom, found in central and eastern Texas from the Red River south to the Brazos River drainage.

Description: olive green back fading to silvery-white or pale, brassy sides and belly; adipose fin; blunt snout; black stripe through center of deeply forked tail

Similar Species: Threadfin Shad (pg. 56)

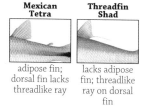

| **Mexican Tetra** | **Threadfin Shad** |
| adipose fin; dorsal fin lacks threadlike ray | lacks adipose fin; threadlike ray on dorsal fin |

MEXICAN TETRA

Astyanax mexicanus

Other Names: sardinita mexicana

Habitat: lives in a variety of habitats, including rivers, wetlands and backwaters; prefers clear, shallow, flowing water and gravel bottom; seldom found in deep or weedy water

Range: subtropical America including the lower Rio Grande and Pecos rivers in Texas and New Mexico, introduced elsewhere; in Texas, native to the Nueces, Pecos and Rio Grande drainages, introduced elsewhere by "bucket biologists"

Food: fish, aquatic and terrestrial insects, snails, crayfish, filamentous algae and other plant matter

Reproduction: fish hatched in spring mature by first autumn; spawns year-round in suitable tropical habitat, late spring to early summer in cooler northern waters; adhesive eggs hatch in 24 hours

Average Size: up to 4¾ inches

Records: none

Notes: The Mexican Tetra belongs to a large family of about 800 species found mostly in Central and South America and Africa. It is closely related to the Minnow family but distinguishable by its adipose fin and toothy jaws. May form dense schools that blacken the water. Most introductions are believed to be the results of bait-bucket releases; in Texas, Tetras do well in springs with constant water temperature and flow and make an excellent aquarium fish.

RIO GRANDE CICHLID

MOZAMBIQUE TILAPIA

Description: olive to bluish-black coloration with cream and turquoise spots; 4 to 6 dark blotches on sides; long, tapered dorsal and anal fins; 5 to 7 spines in anal fin

Similar Species: Bluegill (pg. 156), Mozambique Tilapia

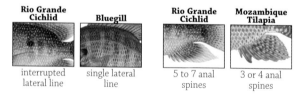

Rio Grande Cichlid	Bluegill	Rio Grande Cichlid	Mozambique Tilapia
interrupted lateral line	single lateral line	5 to 7 anal spines	3 or 4 anal spines

RIO GRANDE CICHLID

Cichlasoma cyanoguttatum

Other Names: Rio Grande perch, Texas cichlid, mojarra de Norta

Habitat: lakes, large springs and rivers, generally with water temperatures above 49 degrees

Range: native to tropical and subtropical America, northwest Mexico and southern Texas, introduced in a number of states but established in few due to its need for warm water; in Texas, native to the lower Rio Grande drainage, but is now also found on the Edwards Plateau in the Colorado, Guadalupe, San Antonio and San Marcos rivers

Food: small fish, crustaceans, insects, fish eggs

Reproduction: spawns in spring, over rocky bottom; both parents guard eggs and young

Average Size: up to 6 inches

Records: State—1 pound, 9 ounces, South Llano River, 2001; North American—1 pound, 5 ounces, Concho River, Texas, 1996

Notes: The only cichlid native to the United States, it is popular with anglers in some areas of its range such as Florida and Louisiana, and is commonly called the Rio Grande perch. Though its average size is small, it fights hard and makes good table fare. Similar in appearance to the non-native Mozambique Tilapia, it is primarily found in the Guadalupe, San Antonio, and San Marcos drainages.

Description: gray back with purple or bronze reflections; silver sides; white underbelly; humped back; dorsal fin extends from hump to near tail; lateral line runs from head through the tail

Similar Species: Striped Bass (pg. 172)

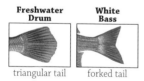

Freshwater Drum	White Bass
triangular tail	forked tail

FRESHWATER DRUM

Aplodinotus grunniens

Other Names: croaker, gaspergou, grinder, sheepshead, thunderpumper

Habitat: slow-to-moderate current areas of rivers and streams; shallow lakes with soft bottoms; prefers turbid (cloudy) water

Range: Hudson Bay, Canada through the Midwest and eastern Mexico; widespread in Texas except in the Panhandle

Food: small fish, insects, crayfish, clams

Reproduction: spawns in April and May at water temperatures are above 64 to 66 degrees; schools of drum scatter and fertilize eggs in open water over sand or gravel; a female may produce up to 600,000 eggs; no nest or parental care

Average Size: 12 to 20 inches, 12 ounces to 5 pounds

Records: State—34 pounds, 11 ounces, Lake Texoma, 1995; North American—54 pounds, 8 ounces, Nickajack Lake, Tennessee, 1972

Notes: The only member of the drum family found strictly in freshwater, this species gets its name from the grunting noise males produce primarily to attract females. This odd sound is made by vibrating muscles against the swim bladder. Though considered a rough fish by many anglers, the Freshwater Drum is a hard fighter and its flaky white flesh is tasty, but dries out easily due to its low oil content. Sometimes caught by anglers casting or trolling for other species, it can also be taken on live bait fished on bottom.

Description: dark brown on top with yellow sides and a white belly; long, snake-like body with large mouth; pectoral fins; gill slits; continuous dorsal, tail and anal fin

Similar Species: none

AMERICAN EEL

Anguilla rostrata

Other Names: common or freshwater eel

Habitat: soft bottoms of medium to large streams; brackish tidewater areas

Range: Atlantic Ocean, eastern and central North America and eastern Central America; native to most of Texas but currently eliminated from many central and western waters due to the construction of dams

Food: insects, crayfish, small fish

Reproduction: a "catadromous" species which spends most of its life in freshwater and returns to the Sargasso Sea in the North Atlantic Ocean to spawn; females lay up to 20 million eggs; adults die after spawning

Average Size: 24 to 36 inches, 1 to 3 pounds

Records: State—6 pounds, 7 ounces, Lady Bird Lake, 2001; North American—8 pounds, 8 ounces, Cliff Pond, Massachusetts, 1992

Notes: Leaf-shaped larval eels drift with ocean currents for about a year. When they reach the river mouths of North and Central America, they develop into small eels (elvers). Males remain in estuaries; females migrate far upstream, reportedly crawling along shore or over concrete dams when possible to bypass obstructions. At maturity (up to 20 years of age), adults return to the Sargasso Sea. Rarely seen, the American Eel is most active at night, often resting under rocks, sunken logs and other cover during the day.

Description: brown to dark olive back and sides fading to white or yellowish belly; long, cylindrical body; short, broad snout; large teeth; diamond-shaped, interlocking scales

Similar Species: Longnose Gar (pg. 48), Shortnose Gar (pg. 50), Spotted Gar (pg. 52)

Alligator Gar	**Longnose Gar**	**Shortnose Gar**	**Spotted Gar**
two rows of large teeth on either side of upper jaw	lacks two rows of large teeth on either side of upper jaw	lacks two rows of large teeth on either side of upper jaw	lacks two rows of large teeth on either side of upper jaw

ALLIGATOR GAR
Atractosteus spatula

Other Names: gator gar

Habitat: sluggish pools and backwaters of streams; lakes and ponds; tolerates brackish conditions

Range: Gulf of Mexico drainages north to Ohio and Missouri river systems, isolated population in Nicaragua; in Texas, rivers and streams from the Red River to Rio Grande

Food: fish, crustaceans, waterbirds

Reproduction: matures at about age 6; spawns in spring from April into June; female may produce up to 100,000 adhesive eggs

Average Size: up to 200 pounds and 9 feet long

Records: State and North American—279 pounds, Rio Grande River, Texas, 1951

Notes: The largest member of the gar family, this freshwater leviathan can attain lengths of more than 9 feet and can weigh more than 300 pounds. Though traditionally disdained by anglers, the Alligator Gar offers great sport and is pursued by a growing number of archers and hook-and-line fishermen. The latter group often uses baits with nylon threads to entangle the gar's sharp teeth.

Description: dark olive to brown back and upper sides, fading to white belly; long, cylindrical body; hard, plate-like scales; long snout in comparison to its width

Similar Species: Shortnose Gar (pg. 50), Spotted Gar (pg. 52)

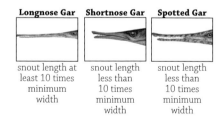

Longnose Gar	Shortnose Gar	Spotted Gar
snout length at least 10 times minimum width	snout length less than 10 times minimum width	snout length less than 10 times minimum width

LONGNOSE GAR

Lepisosteus osseus

Other Names: billfish, billy or needlenose gar

Habitat: floodplain lakes, moderately clear streams, river backwaters and oxbows, reservoirs

Range: central U.S. through the Mississippi drainage south into Mexico; statewide in Texas

Food: fish

Reproduction: spawns over riffles or in weedy shallows of lakes during spring at water temperatures of about 64 to 69 degrees; while attended by one or more males, female lays up to 70,000 green eggs, which hatch in 6 to 9 days; newly hatched gar use disks on their snouts to attach themselves to nearby plants, rocks or timber until the mouth and digestive tract form enough to allow feeding

Average Size: 24 to 36 inches, 2 to 5 pounds

Records: State and North American—50 pounds, 5 ounces, Trinity River, Texas, 1954

Notes: A modified swim bladder allows the Longnose Gar to gulp air at the surface, enabling it to tolerate oxygen levels too low for most other fish. An efficient predator that primarily targets fish, it will eat a variety of species but studies have shown Gizzard Shad are commonly on their menu.

Description: olive to slate-green back and sides fading to whitish belly; dark spots on rear third of body; long, cylindrical profile; hard, diamond-shaped scales

Similar Species: Longnose Gar (pg. 48), Spotted Gar (pg. 52)

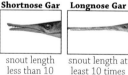

Shortnose Gar	**Longnose Gar**
snout length less than 10 times minimum width	snout length at least 10 times minimum width

Shortnose Gar	**Spotted Gar**
lacks dark spots on pectoral and pelvic fins, and top of head	dark spots on pectoral and pelvic fins, and top of head

SHORTNOSE GAR

Lepisosteus platostomus

Other Names: billy, shortbill or stubnose gar

Habitat: open water of large, slow-moving rivers, backwaters and shallow oxbow lakes

Range: Mississippi River drainage from southern Great Lakes to Mexico; in Texas, the Red River basin below Lake Texoma

Food: small fish, crayfish, insects

Reproduction: matures at about 15 inches in length; spawns May into July; eggs are deposited over vegetation or other objects in quiet backwaters; eggs hatch within 8 days

Average Size: 12 to 24 inches, 1 to 3 pounds

Records: State—3 pounds, 14 ounces, Arrowhead, 1995; North American—6 pounds, 6 ounces, Kentucky Lake, Tennessee, 2001

Notes: Preferring somewhat more "active" water than its cousin the Longnose Gar, the Shortnose Gar can also tolerate cloudier conditions. Like the Longnose, it is able to gulp air at the surface to survive low oxygen levels that would kill most other fish. Although its flesh is considered poor table fare, it is sought by archers and some hook-and-line anglers.

Description: dark olive to brown back fading to silver-white sides and white belly; olive-brown to black spots on head, fins and upper body; long, cylindrical body

Similar Species: Longnose Gar (pg. 48), Shortnose Gar (pg. 52)

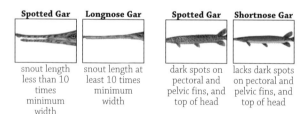

Spotted Gar	Longnose Gar	Spotted Gar	Shortnose Gar
snout length less than 10 times minimum width	snout length at least 10 times minimum width	dark spots on pectoral and pelvic fins, and top of head	lacks dark spots on pectoral and pelvic fins, and top of head

SPOTTED GAR

Lepisosteus oculatus

Other Names: garfish

Habitat: streams, lakes and swamps; prefers clear water with abundant weed growth; occasionally found in brackish water

Range: Mississippi River drainage from lower Ohio River and Lake Erie systems south to Texas and Florida; in Texas, the Red River to Rio Grande basin

Food: fish, crayfish, freshwater shrimp, crabs

Reproduction: spawns April to May in shallow water with weed growth and low flows; attended by several males, female scatters up to 20,000 adhesive green eggs, which often attach to aquatic plants and hatch within 14 days

Average Size: up to 36 inches and 8 pounds

Records: State—9 pounds, 12 ounces, Lake Mexia, 1994; North American—28 pounds, 8 ounces, Lake Seminole, Florida, 1987

Notes: Like other gar, the Spotted Gar has a special swim bladder that allows it to gulp air at the surface, enabling it to survive in poorly oxygenated backwaters. Its eggs are extremely toxic to humans. Though they are voracious predators, Spotted Gar aren't quite at the top of the food chain. Despite their camouflage, careless gar end up in the stomachs of larger fish, snakes, herons and alligators.

Description: silvery-blue back with white sides and belly; small mouth; last rays of dorsal fin form a long thread; deep body; young fish have a dark spot behind the gill flap

Similar Species: Threadfin Shad (pg. 56)

Gizzard Shad	Threadfin Shad	Gizzard Shad	Threadfin Shad
lower jaw does not project past tip of snout	lower jaw projects past tip of snout	no yellow on tail	yellow tail

GIZZARD SHAD
Dorosoma cepedianum

Other Names: hickory, mud or jack shad, skipjack

Habitat: quiet water of large rivers, reservoirs, lakes and swamps; brackish and saline waters in coastal areas

Range: the St. Lawrence River and the Great Lakes, Mississippi, Atlantic and Gulf Slope drainages from Quebec to Mexico, south to central Florida, introduced elsewhere; statewide in Texas

Food: plankton, algae, insects and other organic matter

Reproduction: spawns May through June in tributary streams and sheltered bays; mixed schools of males and females roil at the surface, releasing eggs and milt without regard for individual mates; adhesive eggs sink to bottom and hatch in 2 to 7 days

Average Size: 6 to 14 inches, 1 to 16 ounces

Records: State—2 pounds, 10 ounces, Lady Bird Lake, 1997; North American—4 pounds, 12 ounces, Lake Oahe, South Dakota, 2006

Notes: The Gizzard Shad is a prolific species across much of its native and introduced range. The name "gizzard" refers to its long, convoluted intestine, which is often packed with sand. It filters plankton, algae and suspended organic matter through its gill rakers, and also "grazes" the bottom for insects and organic sediment. Large Gizzard Shad up to 18 inches in length are sometimes caught with hook and line, but they have little food value.

Description: silver-blue back fading to white sides and belly; yellow coloration on all fins except dorsal; speckled chin and bottom of mouth

Similar Species: Gizzard Shad (pg. 54)

lower jaw projects past tip of snout

lower jaw does not project past tip of snout

yellow tail

no yellow on tail

THREADFIN SHAD

Dorosoma petenense

Other Names: none

Habitat: open water of large rivers and reservoirs; prefers moderate current in flowing water; seeks warm water when temperatures fall, sometimes schooling along shallow, sandy shorelines

Range: native west of the Appalachians north to Kentucky, west to Texas, south to the Rio Grande drainage and east to Florida, widely introduced; throughout eastern Texas drainages, introduced into numerous reservoirs statewide

Food: planktonic algae and crustaceans, some organic matter from bottom

Reproduction: spawns in spring when water reaches about 70 degrees and may continue through summer; schools follow shorelines, spawning near grass clumps, wood or debris; depending on its size, a female typically carries between 800 to 9,000 adhesive eggs, which hatch in 4 to 5 days

Average Size: 4 to 5 inches

Records: State—2.08 ounces, Richland-Chambers Reservoir, 1998; North American—none

Notes: To say the Threadfin Shad is prolific is an understatement. It forms a large part of the forage base in many systems. Despite its reproductive potential, it is extremely sensitive to temperature, and massive die-offs can occur at temperatures below 45 degrees. Commonly used as baitfish by anglers.

Description: olive-brown back; sides tan, yellow to black fading to yellowish-white underside; sides marked by series of thin, dark bars; broad, flat head; breeding males may turn bright yellow and red

Similar Species: Mosquitofish (pg. 64)

Plains Killifish	**Mosquitofish**	**Plains Killifish**	**Mosquitofish**
vertical bars on sides	sides lack bars	front of dorsal fin slightly ahead of anal fin	anal fin almost entirely ahead of dorsal fin

PLAINS KILLIFISH

Fundulidae

Fundulus zebrinus

Other Names: none

Habitat: rivers and shallow streams, often with a sand or silt bottom; favors quiet water adjacent to shoals, channels and banks; also found in backwaters; tolerates some current

Range: native to Mississippi River and Gulf Slope drainages from Missouri to Wyoming south to Texas, introduced elsewhere; found in west and northwest Texas

Food: aquatic invertebrates, algae

Reproduction: matures at about 2 years; spawns May through July when water temperatures reach 80 degrees; males do not establish territories but become aggressive toward other males; spawns in pairs, commonly burying eggs in sand

Average Size: 2 to 3 inches

Records: none

Notes: A common species on the western Great Plains, the Plains Killifish can survive in water less than an inch deep and tolerate water temperatures approaching 90 degrees. A true diehard, it has been known to survive in areas where farm runoff has left the bottom covered with oxygen-burning organic matter. Lives in loose schools and has been observed burying itself in sand, leaving only its head exposed.

CHESTNUT LAMPREY

SOUTHERN BROOK LAMPREY

Description: yellowish-tan to greenish-gray back and upper sides; eel-like body; mouth is a large, round sucking disk

Similar Species: American Eel (pg. 44), Southern Brook Lamprey

Chestnut Lamprey	American Eel	Chestnut Lamprey	Southern Brook Lamprey
mouth is a sucking disk	mouth has jaws	when extended, mouth is wider than head	when extended, mouth is narrower than head

CHESTNUT LAMPREY

Ichthyomyzon castaneus

Other Names: bloodsucker, hitchhiker, lamper, seven-eyed cat

Habitat: large streams, rivers and reservoirs

Range: central Manitoba south through Red River drainage to Mississippi and Great Lakes basins to the Gulf Slope; in Texas, it occurs in eastern lakes and waterways of the Neches, Red and Sabine drainages

Food: young are filter feeders of organic matter in stream bottoms; adults are parasitic, feeding on the blood of host fish

Reproduction: matures in second spring after transformation from larval stage; spawns in nests on gravel bottom in creeks and rivers; spawning typically reported in April or May; numerous lampreys may spawn in a single nest

Average Size: 10 to 12 inches

Records: none

Notes: Lampreys differ from true fishes in that they lack jaws and paired fins, and possess gill pockets instead of standard gills. These eel-like, primitive creatures inspire disgust or dislike among humans, perhaps because of the destruction caused by the non-native Sea Lamprey to Great Lakes fisheries. Still, native lampreys coexist with Lone Star fish populations. The Chestnut Lamprey is parasitic on fish, but the related Southern Brook Lamprey (*Ichthyomyzon gagei*) is not.

Description: olive back and upper sides, fading to whitish or yellow below; may have rows of dusky spots on side; 10 to 12 rays in relatively small dorsal fin; small head and mouth

Similar Species: Sailfin Molly

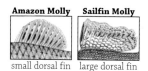

Amazon Molly **Sailfin Molly**

small dorsal fin   large dorsal fin

AMAZON MOLLY

Poecilia formosa

Other Names: none

Habitat: slow-flowing streams, ditches, backwaters and sloughs

Range: central Texas to Veracruz, Mexico; native to the lower Rio Grande in Texas, introduced in Nueces, San Antonio and San Marcos rivers

Food: algae and other vegetable matter, zooplankton, invertebrates

Reproduction: matures in 1 to 6 months; broods of up to 100 young (usually around 30) are produced when female breeds with male of closely related members of the genus *Poecilia*

Average Size: up to 3¾ inches

Records: none

Notes: The Amazon Molly is an amazing all-female species that survives by breeding with males of other *Poecilia* species—only one of which, the Sailfin Molly, is found in Texas. In a process known as gynogenesis, the female Amazon Molly produces eggs that are activated by the sperm of a related species, but no inherited traits are passed along from the male. As a result, the daughters are genetic copies of their mother.

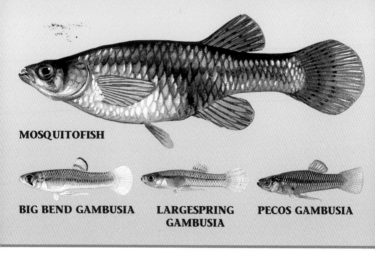

MOSQUITOFISH

BIG BEND GAMBUSIA   LARGESPRING   PECOS GAMBUSIA
                        GAMBUSIA

Description: gray to brown or olive with no bars or bands on sides; rounded tail; flat head; mouth pointed upward

Similar Species: Plains Killifish (pg. 58)

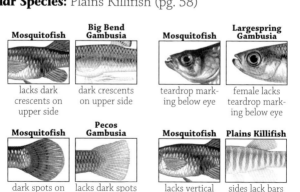

Mosquitofish	Big Bend Gambusia	Mosquitofish	Largespring Gambusia
lacks dark crescents on upper side	dark crescents on upper side	teardrop marking below eye	female lacks teardrop marking below eye

Mosquitofish	Pecos Gambusia	Mosquitofish	Plains Killifish
dark spots on tail	lacks dark spots on tail	lacks vertical bars on sides	sides lack bars

MOSQUITOFISH

Gambusia affinis

Other Names: western mosquitofish, eastern mosquitofish

Habitat: ponds, oxbows, marshes and backwaters of warm streams and rivers; favors vegetation or other cover, but adapts to a variety of conditions

Range: native to Atlantic and Gulf Slope drainages from southern New Jersey to Mexico, the Mississippi River basin from central Indiana and Illinois south to the Gulf, widely introduced; statewide in Texas

Food: zooplankton, invertebrates, small fish

Reproduction: gives birth to live young; breeding season lasts 10 to 15 weeks in summer; female may produce 4 broods per year; eggs hatch after 21 to 28 days

Average Size: males less than 2 inches; females 2 inches

Records: State—2 inches, Canton City, 2007; North American—none

Notes: An aggressive predator, the Mosquitofish has been stocked for mosquito control in many areas outside its native range. However, recent research indicates it is not particularly effective in reducing mosquito populations or the incidence of mosquito-borne diseases. In fact, it may help mosquitoes by reducing competition with zooplankton and mosquito predators. In some habitats, particularly in the West, it displaced native species that are more efficient mosquito killers. Similar to the rare and geographically limited Big Bend, Largespring and Pecos *Gambusia* species.

Description: slate gray back fading to silver sides and white belly; body often has dark blotches; downturned eyes set low on head; upturned mouth lacks barbels

Similar Species: Common Carp (pg. 68), Grass Carp (pg. 70)

Bighead Carp	**Common Carp**
low-set eyes, upturned mouth lacks barbels	eyes high on head; downturned mouth with barbels

Bighead Carp	**Grass Carp**
eye below front of upper lip	eye even with or above front of upper lip

Bighead Carp	**Grass Carp**
anal fin 13-14 rays	anal fin 8-10 rays

BIGHEAD CARP

Hypophthalmichthys nobilis

Other Names: Asian carp

Habitat: large, warm rivers and connected lakes; often found in lower sections of tributaries and in flooded areas

Range: southern and central China, widely introduced in U.S.; in Texas, reported in the Victor Braunig, Kirby and Fort Phantom Hill reservoirs and the Red River below Lake Texoma

Food: floating plankton and organic matter

Reproduction: spawns from late spring to early summer in warm, flowing water, often in conjunction with increases in current or water level

Average Size: 20 to 30 inches; 12 to 15 pounds

Records: State and North American—90 pounds, Kirby Lake, Texas, 2000

Notes: The Bighead Carp is a non-native species that could threaten native fish by competing for (or depleting) plankton. While young fish of many species could be affected, species considered among the most at risk for competition by Bighead Carp include the Paddlefish, the Bigmouth Buffalo and the Gizzard Shad. Emptying bait buckets on land and draining livewells before heading to a new lake are two easy ways to help stop the spread of exotic species like the Bighead Carp. The Bighead arrived in the U.S. in the early 1970s, imported by a fish farmer hoping to improve water quality.

COMMON CARP

MIRROR CARP

KOI

Description: brassy yellow to golden brown or dark olive sides; white belly; some red on tail and anal fin; each scale has a dark spot at the base and a dark margin; two pairs of barbels near round, extendable mouth

Similar Species: Bighead Carp (pg. 66), Grass Carp (pg. 70)

Common Carp

downturned mouth with barbels

Bighead Carp

upturned mouth lacks barbels

Grass Carp

forward facing mouth lacks barbels

COMMON CARP

Cyprinus carpio

Other Names: German, leather or mirror carp, buglemouth

Habitat: warm, shallow, weedy waters of streams and lakes

Range: native to Asia, widely introduced elsewhere; statewide in Texas

Food: prefers insects, crustaceans and mollusks but at times eats algae and other plants

Reproduction: spawns from late February to July in shallow water along stream and lake edges; eggs randomly cast over rocks, logs and debris; spawning adults are easily seen due to energetic splashing along shore; female may produce from 100,000 to 2 million eggs

Average Size: 15 to 22 inches, 1 to 7 pounds

Records: State—43 pounds, 2 ounces, Lady Bird Lake, 2006; North American—57 pounds, 13 ounces, Tidal Basin, Washington D.C., 1983

Notes: A fast-growing Asian minnow, it was introduced in North America as a food fish but has since become considered a pest. It is very prolific and often uproots aquatic plants and increases turbidity (cloudiness) in shallow lakes, causing a decline in waterfowl and native fish populations that require clean water. The Common Carp is not popular with most Lone Star anglers, but some fish for it with nymphs, streamers and natural baits. Mirror Carp and Koi are varieties of the Common Carp.

Description: gold to olive or silver back fading to yellowish-white underside; thick body; broad, blunt head; large, forward-facing mouth; large, dark-edged scales; low-set eyes

Similar Species: Bighead Carp (pg. 66), Common Carp (pg. 68)

Grass Carp	**Bighead Carp**	**Grass Carp**	**Common Carp**
anal fin 8-10 rays	anal fin 13-14 rays	forward facing mouth lacks barbels	downturned mouth with barbels

GRASS CARP
Ctenopharyngodon idella

Other Names: white amur

Habitat: quiet waters of lakes, ponds, and the pools and backwaters of large rivers

Range: native to Asia, eastern Russia and China to the West River in southern China and Thailand, widely introduced in North America; statewide in Texas

Food: aquatic vegetation including filamentous algae

Reproduction: spawns when water temperatures reach 53 to 63 degrees; eggs drift with the current and must remain suspended during incubation, which lasts 20 to 40 hours; for this reason, long stretches of flowing water are required

Average Size: 16 to 40 inches, 5 to 50 pounds

Records: State—53 pounds, 8 ounces, Toledo Bend Reservoir, 2006; North American—78 pounds, 12 ounces, Flint River, Georgia, 2003

Notes: The Grass Carp is an herbivore with a voracious appetite, known to consume from 40 to 300 percent of its body weight each day. It is also one of the largest members of the minnow family, reportedly reaching 48 inches and weighing well over 100 pounds in its native range. It has been stocked in North America as a food fish and to control aquatic vegetation. Because it eats plants, it is rarely caught on hook and line. Texas Grass Carp fisheries include sterile "triploids" (fish with 3 sets of chromosomes rather than two) along with fertile, reproducing fish.

CREEK CHUB

SUCKERMOUTH MINNOW

Description: grayish-green to bronze back; silver to white or yellowish sides and belly; fins may develop an orange coloration on breeding fish

Similar Species: Suckermouth Minnow

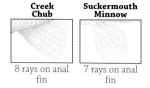

Creek Chub — 8 rays on anal fin

Suckermouth Minnow — 7 rays on anal fin

CREEK CHUB

Semotilus atromaculatus

Cyprinidae

Other Names: brook or common chub, horned dace

Habitat: small to medium-size streams and rivers with gravel, sand or rubble bottom; tolerates turbid (cloudy) conditions but prefers clear water

Range: eastern U.S. and southeastern Canada from Manitoba south through Colorado into Texas; found in East Texas and the lower Brazos River basin

Food: insects, small fish, fish eggs, crayfish, worms, mollusks

Reproduction: spawns in water temperatures of 55 to 65 degrees; male builds and guards nest in gravel above or below a riffle, or at the lower end of a pool in moderate current; when complete, the nest is a short ridge of stones with a shallow pit on the downstream end; female deposits 25 to 50 eggs at a time; male covers fertilized eggs

Average Size: 7 to 12 inches, 8 to 12 ounces

Records: none

Notes: The Creek Chub is a food source for many predators. Large adults are solitary, often hiding beneath undercut banks or roots; small chubs school with other minnows. Male defends the nest by using its head to strike intruders. Similar in appearance to Suckermouth Minnow (*Phenacobius mirabilis*) found in Canadian, Colorado, Red, Sabine and Trinity drainages.

Description: tan to brown back; silver sides; flattened snout overhangs large mouth; barbel at corner of mouth; broad, wedge-shaped head

Similar Species: Golden Shiner (pg. 94)

Flathead Chub	Golden Shiner	Flathead Chub	Golden Shiner
small barbel in corner of mouth	lacks barbel in corner of mouth	8 rays on anal fin	11 to 15 rays on anal fin

FLATHEAD CHUB

Platygobio gracilis

Other Names: none

Habitat: main branches of turbid (cloudy) streams and rivers; often found in fast current with sand or gravel bottom; also occurs in pools of small, clear streams

Range: the Mackenzie, Saskatchewan and Lake Winnipeg drainages in Canada south through the Plains states bordering the Rocky Mountains to New Mexico, Texas and Arkansas; in Texas, found in the Canadian River basin

Food: terrestrial and aquatic invertebrates, algae

Reproduction: matures at 2 years; spawns in summer; little is known about spawning behavior

Average Size: 4 to 10 inches

Records: none

Notes: The Flathead Chub ranges from the Yukon to Texas and New Mexico, giving it one of the widest north-south distributions in the *Cyprinidae* family. Studies indicate the Flathead Chub relies heavily on external taste buds to locate food, and may be outcompeted by sight predators such as shiners. This may help explain its fondness for cloudy water conditions. It is an active fish, often moving in mixed schools with other minnow species.

Description: olive to brown or black back, fading to white or yellowish underneath; may have dark blotches on sides, and dark stripe ahead of eye; upper jaw and snout extend well beyond lower jaw; small barbel in corner of mouth; breeding males develop reddish-orange on head and fins

Similar Species: Suckermouth Minnow (pg. 72)

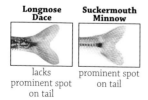

Longnose Dace
lacks prominent spot on tail

Suckermouth Minnow
prominent spot on tail

LONGNOSE DACE

Rhinichthys cataractae

Other Names: none

Habitat: prefers stream riffles with rubble or gravel bottom; also found in lakes

Range: northern North America from the Arctic Circle in the Mackenzie River drainage south to Georgia, also in the Rocky Mountains south into Texas and Mexico; found in southwest Texas in the Rio Grande drainage to Laredo

Food: aquatic invertebrates (immature insects picked from rocks), algae, fish eggs

Reproduction: matures in about 3 years; spawns over gravel bottom in shallow riffles when water temperature reaches about 53 degrees in late spring or early summer

Average Size: 3 to 5 inches

Records: none

Notes: A widespread little fish across its continental range, the Longnose Dace is an important forage species for large predators. It is well-suited to darting among stones in swift-flowing streams. It feeds primarily on immature insects. Highly adaptable, it can survive in a variety of water conditions from clear to turbid (cloudy).

Description: olive back fading to silvery white belly; darkly outlined scales; dark to dusky stripe on side, separated from dark spot on tail; dark spot on dorsal fin; stout body; rounded snout; large eye

Similar Species: Fathead Minnow (pg. 80)

Bullhead Minnow

dark crescent on snout between upper lip and nostril

Fathead Minnow

lacks dark crescent on snout between upper lip and nostril

Bullhead Minnow

prominent spot on base of tail

Fathead Minnow

lacks prominent spot on base of tail

BULLHEAD MINNOW

Pimephales vigilax

Other Names: none

Habitat: slow-moving pools and backwaters of midsized to large streams; also found in lakes, bayous, scour holes and ditches; tolerates silty and turbid (cloudy) conditions but is seldom found in strong current; prefers sand or silt bottom

Range: the Mississippi River drainage from Minnesota south to Mexico eastward through the Gulf Slope drainages to Georgia; statewide in Texas

Food: insects, crustaceans, also algae, seeds and other plant matter

Reproduction: spawns late spring throughout summer; male excavates nest under rocks, tree branches, or other items; female deposits a cluster of eggs in a single layer on the underside of the object; male guards nest and uses a fleshy patch on its back to keep sediments off the eggs, which typically hatch in 4 to 6 days

Average Size: up to 1 to 3 inches

Records: none

Notes: A schooling fish often found with other minnows and shiner species, the Bullhead Minnow typically feeds on or near bottom. If you're in doubt about whether you have a Fathead or Bullhead Minnow, check the inside of the fish. Bullhead Minnows have a light silvery body cavity lining and relatively short S-shaped intestine; Fathead Minnows have dark linings and long intestines with multiple loops.

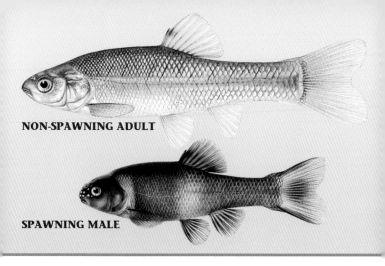

NON-SPAWNING ADULT

SPAWNING MALE

Description: olive back, golden yellow sides and white belly; dark lateral line widens to spot at base of tail; rounded snout and fins; no scales on head; dark blotch on dorsal fin

Similar Species: Bullhead Minnow (pg. 78)

Fathead Minnow	Bullhead Minnow	Fathead Minnow	Bullhead Minnow
lacks dark crescent on snout between upper lip and nostril	dark crescent on snout between upper lip and nostril	lacks prominent spot on base of tail	prominent spot on base of tail

Cyprinidae

FATHEAD MINNOW
Pimephales promelas

Other Names: blackhead, mudminnow, tuffy

Habitat: streams, ponds and lakes, particularly shallow, weedy or turbid (cloudy) areas lacking predators

Range: native to much of North America from Quebec to the Northwest Territories south to Alabama, Texas and New Mexico, widely introduced elsewhere; statewide in Texas

Food: primarily algae and other plant matter, but will eat insects and copepods

Reproduction: when water temperature reaches 65 degrees, male prepares nest under rocks or sticks; female enters, turns upside down and lays adhesive eggs on the overhang; the male fertilizes and guards the eggs, and massages them with a special, mucus-like pad on his back

Average Size: 3 to 4 inches

Records: none

Notes: A widespread fish commonly used as bait, the Fathead Minnow is hardy and withstands extremely high temperatures and low oxygen levels. Prior to spawning, the male or "bull" develops a dark coloration, breeding tubercles on its head that resemble small horns and a mucus-like patch on its back; during this phase, anglers report having better luck when using female Fatheads, perhaps due to their color or differing scent. Some biologists believe the Fathead Minnow threatens native fish in areas where it has been introduced.

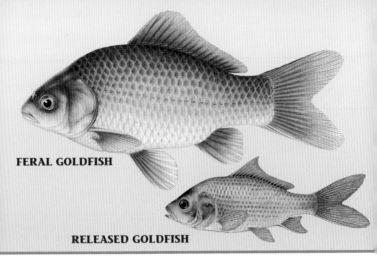

FERAL GOLDFISH

RELEASED GOLDFISH

Description: feral (wild)—back and upper sides dark olive-brown fading to yellow or lighter below; domestic—orange or red coloration; both variations have long dorsal fin; stocky, compressed body

Similar Species: Common Carp (pg. 68), Grass Carp (pg. 70)

Goldfish	Common Carp
forward facing mouth lacks barbels	downturned mouth with barbels

Goldfish	Grass Carp
dorsal fin 15-19 rays	dorsal fin 7-9 rays

GOLDFISH
Carassius auratus

Other Names: none

Habitat: ponds and the shallow bays of lakes; pools and backwater areas of streams and rivers

Range: native to Asia but widely introduced across North America; found statewide in Texas

Food: algae and other plant matter, insects, crustaceans

Reproduction: matures at 1 to 3 years; spawns in late spring and summer, scattering adhesive eggs over submerged vegetation, roots or other objects; female may produce 400,000 eggs, which hatch in 5 to 6 days

Average Size: up to 16 inches and 3 pounds

Records: State—5 pounds, Lake Conroe, 1994; North American—3 pounds, 2 ounces, Lourdes Pond, Indiana, 2002

Notes: A non-native species, the Goldfish has been widely introduced in Texas due to releases of bait and aquarium fish. Those released from fish bowls and minnow buckets are typically orange or red in color, but second-generation "wild" or feral Goldfish often lose this trademark coloration and look very similar to Common Carp. Spawning patterns are also similar to Common Carp, making hybrids common in waters where both species are well-established.

NON-SPAWNING ADULT

SPAWNING MALE

Description: silver to light brown back and sides with scattered dark spots; white to silver belly; moderately stout body; bulbous snout overhanging mouth; fleshy lower lip partially covering hard shelf-like lower jaw; mature males have dark stripe along lower half of dorsal fin

Similar Species: Mexican Stoneroller (pg. 86)

Central Stoneroller

typically 47 to 55 lateral line scales

Mexican Stoneroller

typically 58 to 77 lateral line scales

CENTRAL STONEROLLER

Campostoma anomalum

Other Names: none

Habitat: pools and riffles, mainly in permanent streams but occasionally in Plains streams with intermittent flows; prefers sand, gravel or bedrock bottoms

Range: Colorado, Wyoming and northern Mexico north to Minnesota, east to the Appalachians; in Texas, found mainly on the Edwards Plateau, but also in rivers including the Brazos, Colorado and Red

Food: plant debris and algae on stream bottoms, also aquatic insects

Reproduction: spawns February through July; male constructs pit-type nest in shallow pools or riffles on fine gravel adjacent to deeper water, often rolling small stones in the process; female deposits adhesive eggs in the pit, which the male fertilizes and covers

Average Size: 3 to 7 inches

Records: none

Notes: A fascinating species, the Central Stoneroller uses the odd, blade-like extension of its lower jaw to scrape algae and other plant matter from objects such as rocks and logs. It often forms large schools, which can be seen swirling in pools and runs as individual fish "graze" on bottom. Known to leap clear out of the water for no apparent reason, particularly on warm days in spring and fall.

85

Description: back dark gray to olive, fading on sides with scattered dark spots and dark lateral band; white belly; large head with rounded snout and small mouth; lower jaw has hard, shelf-like extension; moderately stout body; breeding males develop darkened and orange areas on dorsal fin

Similar Species: Central Stoneroller (pg. 84)

Mexican Stoneroller

typically 58 to 77 lateral line scales

Central Stoneroller

typically 47 to 55 lateral line scales

MEXICAN STONEROLLER

Campostoma ornatum

Cyprinidae

Other Names: none

Habitat: riffles, runs and areas of pools with some current; prefers bottom of gravel or small rocks in riffles and runs, sand or gravel in pools, and undercut banks or other cover

Range: Rio Yaqui drainage of Mexico, east to Texas, south through Sonora, Chihuahua and Durango, Mexico; in Texas, the Rio Grande system

Food: plant debris, algae, aquatic insects

Reproduction: not well-documented; some sources report spawning activities from winter through late spring; male excavates long, pit-type nest; breeding males develop horn-like tubercles on the head, which are used to defend the nest and stimulate spawning behavior in females; non-adhesive eggs are defended by the male until hatching

Average Size: up to 5 inches

Records: none

Notes: An interesting little native minnow, the Mexican Stoneroller is related to the Central Stoneroller (*Campostoma anomalum*), a widespread species found from northern Mexico and Texas to Minnesota. Both of these species use an odd, blade-like extension of the lower jaw to scrape algae and other plant matter from rocks, logs and other objects on the bottom.

Description: overall silvery coloration; yellowish-olive back fading to silver on sides and silvery white belly; small mouth; 8 rays in anal fin

Similar Species: Flathead Chub (pg. 74), Plains Minnow (pg. 90)

Mississippi Silvery Minnow	**Flathead Chub**	**Mississippi Silvery Minnow**	**Plains Minnow**
lacks barbel in corner of mouth	small barbel in corner of mouth	eye diameter is greater than width of mouth	eye diameter is less than width of mouth

MISSISSIPPI SILVERY MINNOW

Hybognathus nuchalis

Other Names: none

Habitat: streams and small rivers with slow to moderate flows; favors backwaters and pools with sand or silty bottom, avoiding strong current; does not tolerate long spells of extremely turbid (cloudy) conditions

Range: the Mississippi River basin from Texas to Minnesota, east to Alabama, also Rio Grande drainage of New Mexico and Texas; in Texas, eastern streams from the Brazos River north to the Red River and Pecos-Rio Grande watershed

Food: algae and other organic matter scoured from the bottom

Reproduction: spawns January through April in quiet waters along stream banks and in overflow pools and backwaters

Average Size: 3 to 5 inches

Records: none

Notes: The Mississippi Silvery Minnow is often found in large schools near the bottom, where it frequently shares its living space with the Bullhead Minnow and various shiners such as the Weed Shiner. Texas populations are most common in tributaries to the Brazos River but not in the main river itself.

Description: back and upper sides dark greenish-gray; brassy sides; faint to dark lateral stripe; cream-colored belly; overall silvery appearance; pointed dorsal has 8 rays; complete lateral line; small mouth

Similar Species: Flathead Chub (pg. 74), Mississippi Silvery Minnow (pg. 88)

Plains Minnow

lacks barbel in corner of mouth

Flathead Chub

small barbel in corner of mouth

Plains Minnow

eye diameter is less than width of mouth

Mississippi Silvery Minnow

eye diameter is greater than width of mouth

PLAINS MINNOW

Cyprinidae

Hybognathus placitus

Other Names: none

Habitat: eddies, backwaters and main channel edges in rivers; also found in pools below diversion projects

Range: Plains States from Montana through Texas; found in northern Texas, in Canadian, Colorado and Red river basins

Food: algae and other plant matter

Reproduction: matures at 1 year; spawns during high water in spring and summer, usually in turbid (cloudy) conditions; buoyant, non-adhesive eggs tumble downstream with the current

Average Size: 3 to 5 inches

Records: none

Notes: A schooling fish that lives near the bottom, often congregating with various shiners and chubs, the Plains Minnow has not been highly studied. It is thought to feed on algae and other organic matter from the bottom. It has a lengthy spawning season, with repeated spawning bouts triggered by rising water levels from rainfall.

Description: light olive back fading to silvery sides and white belly; large black spot at base of tail; pointed snout; small mouth; lacks barbels; spawning males develop bluish coloration

Similar Species: Suckermouth Minnow (pg. 72)

Blacktail Shiner

snout pointed, forward-facing mouth

Suckermouth Minnow

snout rounded, downward-facing mouth

BLACKTAIL SHINER

Cyprinella venusta

Other Names: blacktailed shiner

Habitat: small to medium-sized streams and ditches lacking weed cover; prefers areas of current with gravel or sand bottom

Range: Gulf Slope from Texas to Florida; central and eastern Texas from Rio Grande drainage to the Red River

Food: insects, algae, seeds

Reproduction: spawns spring through early fall, in Texas from April to September; female deposits average of 130 to 450 eggs in sheltered, crevice-type areas such as cracks in bridge pilings, beneath rocks or in submerged woody cover including tree roots and logs; male defends spawning area against other males and may deposit sperm there before female lays eggs

Average Size: $2\frac{1}{2}$ to $4\frac{1}{2}$ inches

Records: none

Notes: Often found in schools near the surface or mid-depth regions of the water column, the Blacktail Shiner is thought to feed on food items drifting in the current. Females attract prospective mates by emitting sounds that help males distinguish them from related Red Shiners.

Description: olive green back fading to golden or silvery sides; silver-white belly; deep body; small, upturned mouth; scaleless keel on belly behind pelvic fins; breeding males may develop orange-red tail

Similar Species: Red Shiner (pg. 96)

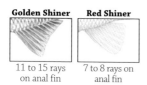

Golden Shiner   Red Shiner

11 to 15 rays on anal fin   7 to 8 rays on anal fin

GOLDEN SHINER

Notemigonus crysoleucas

Other Names: none

Habitat: ponds, lakes, sloughs and slack-water pools in slow-flowing streams; does well in heavy weed growth; tolerates moderately turbid (cloudy) water

Range: central and eastern North America, including Atlantic, Gulf Slope, Great Lakes and Mississippi River basins from Nova Scotia to Alberta south to Texas and Florida, widely introduced; statewide in Texas

Food: plant and animal matter ranging from algae and higher vegetation to crustaceans, insects and snails

Reproduction: spawns in spring and early summer at water temperatures of 70 to 80 degrees; may spawn again in late summer; no nest; female scatters adhesive eggs over vegetation, filamentous algae or nests of other fish such as Largemouth Bass; eggs hatch in 4 days

Average Size: State—8 ounces, Lake Placid, 1996; North American—none

Records: none

Notes: Widely distributed outside its native range due to its status as a bait- and ornamental fish, the Golden Shiner gathers in loose schools from near the surface to the middle of the water column. Some studies have suggested that the Golden Shiner competes with trout and has led to a decline in trout growth and reproduction. Shiners may also compete for food with juvenile bass and sunfish.

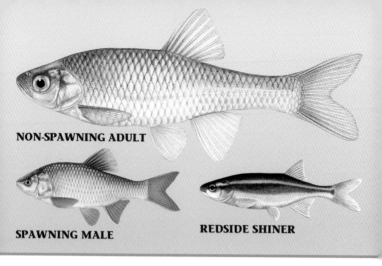

NON-SPAWNING ADULT

SPAWNING MALE

REDSIDE SHINER

Description: olive green to silver-blue back; silver sides; white underside; breeding males develop metallic blue coloration with bright orange-red on the head and fins (except dorsal)

Similar Species: Golden Shiner (pg. 94)

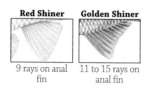

Red Shiner	Golden Shiner
9 rays on anal fin	11 to 15 rays on anal fin

RED SHINER
Cyprinella lutrensis

Other Names: none

Habitat: clear to silty water with fluctuating flows

Range: the mid- to southwestern U.S. from Wisconsin and Indiana west to Colorado, south to Louisiana, Texas and Mexico, widely introduced; statewide in Texas

Food: an opportunist, eats a variety of algae and other plant matter, invertebrates and other small food items

Reproduction: spawns through spring and summer at water temperatures from 60 to 65 degrees; will spawn in a variety of areas, including vegetation and woody cover, over sand and gravel bottoms, even along the edges of nests of other fish (such as Bluegills)

Average Size: up to 3 inches

Records: none

Notes: A schooling fish that spends much of its time in the middle of the water column or near the surface, the Red Shiner can tolerate pollution better than many species. It prefers backwater areas and deep pools where the current volume is less than one foot per second. Nationally, its range has expanded thanks to the bait and aquarium trade. Research has show this highly adaptable fish easily colonizes new areas and hybridizes with "local" shiner species, threatening native fish populations.

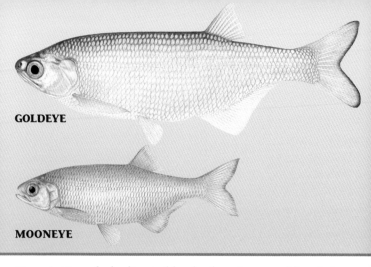

GOLDEYE

MOONEYE

Description: dark olive to blue back and upper sides, fading to silver or golden sides and whitish belly; large scales; large, yellowish eye; fleshy, scaleless keel ahead of pelvic fin

Similar Species: Gizzard Shad (pg. 54), Mooneye

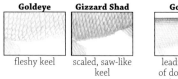

Goldeye	Gizzard Shad
fleshy keel	scaled, saw-like keel

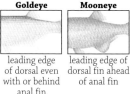

Goldeye	Mooneye
leading edge of dorsal even with or behind anal fin	leading edge of dorsal fin ahead of anal fin

GOLDEYE

Hiodon alosoides

Other Names: toothed or yellow herring, western goldeye

Habitat: large lakes and open water of large rivers, in both quiet pools and swift current

Range: Hudson Bay drainage south to Ohio and Mississippi basins to Louisiana; Red River drainage in Texas, particularly Lake Texoma

Food: aquatic and terrestrial insects, crayfish, fish, snails

Reproduction: spawns in turbid (cloudy) pools and backwaters when water temperatures reach the mid 50s; spawning is not well-documented but believed to occur in middle depths, where eggs and young float freely in the water

Average Size: 14 to 17 inches, 1 to 2 pounds

Records: State—2 pounds, 5 ounces, Lake Texoma, 1996; North American—3 pounds, 13 ounces, Lake Oahe tailwater, South Dakota, 1987

Notes: Closely related to the Mooneye (*Hiodon tergisus*) found in Mississippi basin and sections of the Red River. Thanks to its large, yellow eye and good low-light vision, the Goldeye feeds in the evening and at night, often near the surface. Although it is fun to catch on light tackle and delicious when smoked, it is seldom pursued by anglers.

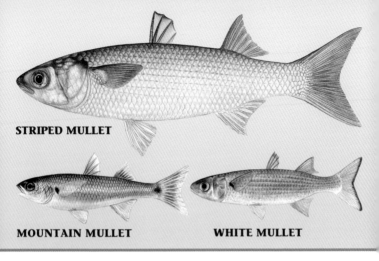

STRIPED MULLET

MOUNTAIN MULLET   **WHITE MULLET**

Description: blue black back fading to silver sides and sil-very-white belly; small, forward-facing mouth; dark spot at base of pectoral fins, which are set high on sides; no visible lateral line

Similar Species: Mountain Mullet, White Mullet

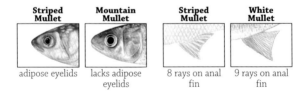

Striped Mullet	Mountain Mullet	Striped Mullet	White Mullet
adipose eyelids	lacks adipose eyelids	8 rays on anal fin	9 rays on anal fin

STRIPED MULLET
Mugil cephalus

Other Names: none

Habitat: freshwater, brackish (slightly salty) and saltwater habitats in depths to nearly 400 feet; prefers water temperatures from 46 to 75 degrees; often schools over sand or mud bottoms

Range: coastal areas, river mouths and estuaries worldwide between 42 degrees N and 42 degrees S latitude; in Texas, coastal waters inland to Lake Texoma

Food: zooplankton, crustaceans, algae, organic debris

Reproduction: males mature at age 3, females mature at age 4; spawns in open sea

Average Size: up to 23 inches and 8 pounds

Records: none

Notes: Primarily a saltwater species, the Striped Mullet is also found in brackish coastal waters and ranges far upstream in freshwater systems such as the lower Mississippi drainage. They can often be spotted leaping from the water to escape predators. Often used as bait by anglers. Not considered a good food fish in Texas waters of the western Gulf of Mexico, where the fillets take on an oily taste, but eaten in other parts of its range.

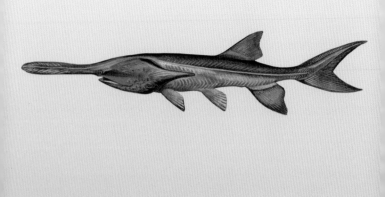

Description: dark bluish-gray to black on back and sides fading to whitish belly; large paddle-like snout; shark-like forked tail

Similar Species: Blue Catfish (pg. 30), Channel Catfish (pg. 32)

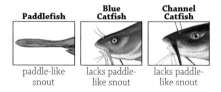

Paddlefish	Blue Catfish	Channel Catfish
paddle-like snout	lacks paddle-like snout	lacks paddle-like snout

PADDLEFISH
Polyodon spathula

Other Names: duckbill, spoonbill, shovelnose cat

Habitat: open water, slow-flowing, deep pools in large rivers and connecting lakes

Range: large rivers of the Mississippi River and adjacent Gulf Coast drainage; in Texas, once widespread in large river systems eastward from the Trinity Basin

Food: plankton

Reproduction: spawns when water levels are rising and water temperatures reach the low 50s; adults migrate from lakes and rivers into streams; breeding schools release eggs over gravel or sand bottom, typically in depths of less than 10 feet; a female may produce up to 600,000 eggs

Average Size: 24 to 48 inches; 30 to 50 pounds

Records: State—none; North American—144 pounds, Dam #7, Kansas, 2004

Notes: Despite its large body size and gaping mouth, the Paddlefish feeds entirely on plankton. It catches these tiny plants and animals by slowly swimming through food-rich areas with its mouth open and filtering the plankton from the water with its gill rakers. It is named for its conspicuous "paddle," which contains a sensory array that helps it locate food. Scientists believe the paddle helps it detect weak electrical fields generated by clouds of plankton.

ORANGETHROAT
DARTER

CYPRESS DARTER

Description: mottled green to yellowish-brown back; dark
bars (blue on male, brown on female); belly orange to
white; dorsal fin and tail red with blue margin; large males
develop blue anal fin, blue to black pelvic fin and two
orange spots at base of tail; thin mark under eye; incom-
plete lateral line; breeding males develop blue and red bars,
bright-orange throat

Similar Species: Cypress Darter

Orangethroat Darter	Cypress Darter
more than 9 porous scales in lateral line	9 or fewer porous scales in lateral line

ORANGETHROAT DARTER

Etheostoma spectabile

Other Names: none

Habitat: most often occurs in small, spring-fed streams with sand, gravel or rocky bottom and no silt, but tolerates turbid (cloudy), warmer conditions

Range: widespread in U.S. central lowlands from southeast Iowa, the southern Great Lakes region and Kentucky south to Texas, west to Colorado; found in central Texas from San Antonio basin to Red River drainage

Food: aquatic invertebrates, small crustaceans, fish eggs

Reproduction: matures at 2 years; spawns in spring and summer; female deposits eggs on gravel bottom in riffles; no further parental care; eggs hatch in 9 to 10 days

Average Size: 1 to $2^1/_2$ inches

Records: none

Notes: One of more than 20 native Texas darters, the Orangethroat is a beautiful little fish, especially during the spawn, when the male sports bluish vertical bars, red blotches and multi-colored fins. Named for its striking orange throat and gill area. Related to Walleye and Yellow Perch but rarely surpasses more than 2 inches in length. Like other darters, it lacks a swim bladder, allowing it to dart quickly from one resting place to another without being swept away by the current.

BIGSCALE LOGPERCH

COMMON LOGPERCH

TEXAS LOGPERCH

Description: olive back; 15 to 20 long, green to black vertical bars on sides, joining stripes on other side of body; stripes on tail and dorsal fins; dark spot on base of tail and under eye; torpedo-shaped body

Similar Species: Common Logperch, Texas Logperch

Bigscale Logperch	Common Logperch	Texas Logperch
vertical bars on sides mostly equal lengths	vertical bars on sides are of differing lengths	vertical bars on sides are of differing lengths

BIGSCALE LOGPERCH

Percina macrolepida

Other Names: none

Habitat: small streams, rivers and reservoirs, often found over sand, gravel or silt bottom in pools and runs

Range: native from the Sabine River, Louisiana, and Red River, Oklahoma, to the Rio Grande basin of Texas, New Mexico and Mexico, introduced in California and Colorado; in Texas, from the Rio Grande to Red and Sabine drainages

Food: reportedly feeds on fish eggs, including centrarchids (bass, sunfish, crappies)

Reproduction: spawns late February through May; spawning is not well-documented, but captive fish have deposited eggs on plant stems

Average Size: 3 to 4 inches

Records: none

Notes: Along with the Dusky Darter, the Bigscale Logperch is considered a "primitive" member of the darter clan, in the genus *Percina*. Thanks to a small air bladder, it spends more time hovering above the bottom than other darters. When introduced beyond its native range, such as in California, it has proven an adaptable invader capable of establishing populations in a variety of habitats.

Description: gray to yellowish-brown back and sides fading to white belly; dark blotches on sides extend below the lateral line; may exhibit some white on lower margin of tail

Similar Species: Walleye (pg. 110)

Saugeye

blotches on sides below lateral line

Walleye

lacks blotches on sides below lateral line

SAUGEYE

Sander vitreus x Sander canadensis

Other Names: sand pike, spotfin

Habitat: large lakes and rivers, often with turbid (cloudy) water

Range: hybrid between Walleye and Sauger, widely stocked in warmwater reservoirs

Food: small fish, aquatic insects, crayfish and other small prey

Reproduction: although it is a hybrid, it occasionally reproduces with Walleye or Sauger

Average Size: 12 to 18 inches, 8 ounces to 2 pounds

Records: State—7 pounds, 12 ounces, Kirby Lake, 1998; North American—15 pounds, 10 ounces, Fort Peck Reservoir, Montana, 1995

Notes: A hybrid of Sauger and Walleye stock reared in hatcheries, the Saugeye is a fast-growing, hard-fighting sport fish that is popular with anglers. Has also been stocked in Texas lakes to help control stunted crappie populations.

Description: dark back with overall silver, golden to dark olive body coloration; white belly; dark spot at base of three last spines in dorsal fin; white spot on bottom lobe of tail; sharp canine teeth

Similar Species: Saugeye (pg. 108), Yellow Perch (pg. 112)

Walleye	**Saugeye**	**Walleye**	**Yellow Perch**
lacks blotches on sides below lateral line	blotches on sides below lateral line	prominent white spot on bottom lobe of tail	no prominent white spot on bottom lobe of tail

WALLEYE
Sander vitreus

Other Names: marble-eyes, walleyed pike, jack

Habitat: large lakes, reservoirs and rivers; lake populations have varied habitat, from near-shore weedbeds to offshore mud flats, rocky structure and basins

Range: originally much of U.S. east of the Rocky Mountains into Canada, now widely stocked; introduced in several Texas impoundments

Food: shad, perch and various minnows, insects, crayfish, leeches and other small prey

Reproduction: mature at 2-4 years; spawns at night in tributary streams and on lake shoals when water temperatures reach 45 to 50 degrees, often in April or early May; small groups of adults spread fertilized eggs; no parental care

Average Size: 14 to 20 inches, 1 to 3 pounds

Records: State—11 pounds, 14 ounces, Lake Meredith, 1990; North American—22 pounds, 11 ounces, Greer's Ferry Lake, Arkansas, 1982

Notes: The Walleye puts up a decent fight, particularly on light tackle, and its flaky, white fillets rank extremely high in table quality. Thanks to a reflective layer of pigment in the eye—the *tapetum lucidum*—the Walleye can see well in low-light conditions. This gives it an advantage over prey species that have poor night vision or cannot quickly adapt to reduced light levels. Walleyes exploit this advantage by feeding in light-reducing conditions such as dusk, dawn, beneath waves, or under thick cloud cover.

Description: 6 to 9 dark, vertical bars on bright yellowish-green to orange background; long dorsal with two distinct lobes; lower fins have a yellow to orange tinge

Similar Species: Walleye (pg. 110)

Yellow Perch	Walleye
lacks large white spot on tail	prominent white spot on tail

YELLOW PERCH

Perca flavescens

Other Names: ringed, striped or jack perch, green hornet

Habitat: warm to cool lakes and slow-flowing streams, adults prefer clear open water

Range: native to Atlantic, Arctic, Great Lakes and Mississippi drainages from southern Canada through North Dakota south and east to Georgia; widely introduced elsewhere, including the Texas Panhandle

Food: small fish, insects, snails, leeches and crayfish

Reproduction: matures at 2 years; spawns at night in shallow, weedy areas in spring when water warms to 45 to 50 degrees; female drapes gelatinous ribbons of eggs over submerged vegetation; eggs incubate 10 to 20 days

Average Size: 8 to 11 inches, 6 to 10 ounces

Records: State—1 pound, .04 ounces, Lake Meredith, 1996; North American—4 pounds, 3 ounces, Bordentown, New Jersey, 1865

Notes: Within their native range, perch are an important link in the food web, serving as forage for Walleyes, Northern Pike, Largemouth Bass and other predators. However, illegally stocked Yellow Perch have had a detrimental effect on native species in some lakes.

Description: olive to dark yellowish-brown back and sides, fading to white or light yellow on belly; dark chain-like marks on sides; dark vertical teardrop mark below eye; fully scaled gill covers; dorsal and anal fins set far back on body

Similar Species: Northern Pike (pg. 118), Redfin Pickerel (pg. 116)

Chain Pickerel

fully scaled gill cover, 4 sensory pores on lower jaw

Northern Pike

scaled upper half of gill cover, 5 sensory pores on lower jaw

Chain Pickerel

chain-like marks on sides

Redfin Pickerel

wavy vertical bars on sides

CHAIN PICKEREL
Esox niger

Other Names: chainside, grass pike, jackfish, mountain trout

Habitat: shallow, weedy lakes, swamps and sluggish streams

Range: Atlantic Slope from Nova Scotia to southern Florida and the Gulf Coast west to Texas, also the Mississippi River basin north to Kentucky and Indiana; in Texas, the Red and Sabine drainages

Food: fish, also crayfish, insects, frogs

Reproduction: spawns when water temperatures reach 45 degrees, typically December to February in Texas; strands of adhesive eggs are deposited on aquatic weed growth; no parental care

Average Size: 24 inches, 3 to 4 pounds

Records: State—4 pounds, 12 ounces, Pat Mayse Lake, 1996; North American—9 pounds, 6 ounces, Homerville, Georgia, 1961

Notes: A toothy predator with a taste for fish, the Chain Pickerel often lies in wait for prey to swim within striking distance. Its namesake chain-link markings help it blend in with its preferred weedy environment. A spirited fighter on light tackle, the pickerel is tasty on the table but somewhat on the bony side. In Lone Star waters, the best pickerel action generally occurs from fall through March or April.

Description: dark olive back, fading to lighter green, brown or bronze sides and white or light yellowish belly; 15 to 36 dark, wavy vertical bars on sides; dark teardrop angled backward; fully scaled gill covers; dorsal and anal fins set far back on body; Redfin Pickerel subspecies—lower fins reddish-orange; Grass Pickerel subspecies—lower fins dusky to yellowish-green

Similar Species: Chain Pickerel (pg. 114), Northern Pike (pg. 118)

Redfin Pickerel	Northern Pike	Redfin Pickerel	Chain Pickerel
fully scaled gill cover, 4 sensory pores on lower jaw	upper half of gill cover scaled, 5 sensory pores on lower jaw	wavy vertical bars on sides	chain-like marks on sides

REDFIN PICKEREL

Esox americanus

Other Names: banded, grass, little or mud pickerel, red-finned pike

Habitat: shallow, weedy lakes, swamps, sluggish streams and backwaters; typically found in heavy weed growth; prefers water temperatures of 75 to 80 degrees

Range: eastern North America from Wisconsin, southern Ontario and Massachusetts to Florida and the Gulf Coast west to Texas; eastern Texas from the Red River system south to the Brazos River drainage

Food: fish, also crayfish, insects, frogs

Reproduction: spawns in spring (sometimes fall and winter as well) when water temperature reaches the high 40s to the low 50s in shallow, weedy water; adhesive eggs are scattered among plants; no parental care

Average Size: up to 12 inches, less than 8 ounces

Records: State—7 ounces, Sam Rayburn Lake, 1996; North American—2 pounds, 10 ounces, Lewis Lake, Georgia, 1982

Notes: Like the Chain Pickerel, the Redfin Pickerel is a toothy predator that feeds heavily on small fish. It is a very scrappy brawler on ultra-light gear, but its small size limits its popularity with anglers. Still, its flaky white fillets are good eating (though bony). There are two recognized subspecies: the Redfin Pickerel (*Esox americanus americanus*) and the Grass Pickerel (*Esox americanus vermiculatus*). Hybridizes with Chain Pickerel and Northern Pike.

117

Description: long body with dorsal fin near tail; head is long and flattened in front, forming a duck-like snout; dark green back, light green sides with bean-shaped light spots; Silver Pike are a rare, silver-colored variant of Northern Pike

Similar Species: Chain Pickerel (pg. 114), Redfin Pickerel (pg. 116)

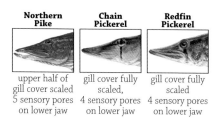

Northern Pike	Chain Pickerel	Redfin Pickerel
upper half of gill cover scaled 5 sensory pores on lower jaw	gill cover fully scaled, 4 sensory pores on lower jaw	gill cover fully scaled 4 sensory pores on lower jaw

NORTHERN PIKE

Esox lucius

Other Names: pickerel, jack, 'gator, hammerhandle, snot rocket

Habitat: lakes, streams and rivers; often found near weeds but ranges in open water; small pike tolerate water temperatures up to 70 degrees; larger fish prefer 55 degrees or less

Range: widespread in northern Europe, Asia and North America; in Texas, introduced in reservoirs in the north

Food: small fish, frogs, crayfish and other small creatures; typically feed on live prey but will scavenge dead fish

Reproduction: spawns late March into April in tributaries and marshes at 34 to 40 degrees; attended by 1-3 males, female deposits eggs in shallow vegetation

Average Size: 18 to 24 inches, 2 to 5 pounds

Records: State—18 pounds, 4 ounces, Lady Bird Lake, 1981; North American—46 pounds, 2 ounces, Sacandaga Reservoir, New York, 1940

Notes: A non-native species, the Northern Pike is a voracious predator and a prized sport fish in its native range. When stocked in new fisheries it can harm native populations. The pike eagerly hits natural and artificial baits and fights hard. It has firm, white flesh and is fine table fare but can acquire a "fishy" taste if fillets contact the outer slime. A daytime sight feeder, it often lies in wait in weedy cover, capturing prey with a fast lunge. Lakes with ample forage, areas of oxygen-rich cool water in summer and low harvest tend to offer the best chance at trophy pike.

RED RIVER PUPFISH

LEON SPRINGS PUPFISH

Description: olive to brownish back and sides fading to white belly; 5 to 8 vertical brown blotches on sides; belly unscaled; deep body with large, flattened connection between tail and body (*caudal peduncle*); large eye

Similar Species: Leon Springs Pupfish, Sheepshead Minnow, (pg. 122)

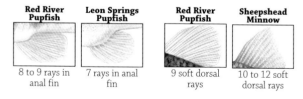

Red River Pupfish	Leon Springs Pupfish	Red River Pupfish	Sheepshead Minnow
8 to 9 rays in anal fin	7 rays in anal fin	9 soft dorsal rays	10 to 12 soft dorsal rays

RED RIVER PUPFISH

Cyprinodon rubrofluviatilis

Other Names: pupfish

Habitat: headwaters, streams and small rivers; favors shallow, shaded runs and pools; tolerates water temperatures well over 100 degrees and salinity three times seawater's

Range: native to upper Red and Brazos River drainages of Texas and Oklahoma, introduced into the Canadian and Colorado river systems

Food: not well documented but believed to be omnivorous, feeding on diatoms and bottom detritus along with algae, small invertebrates, seeds and other organic matter

Reproduction: pupfish spawn in spring and early summer and year-round if water conditions allow and temperatures remain in the high 50s; breeding males become territorial and aggressive; female randomly deposits eggs in male's territory; by patrolling his territory, the male inadvertently guards the eggs, which hatch in several days

Average Size: 2 to $2^{1}/_{4}$ inches

Records: none

Notes: Belongs to the pupfish family, which includes more than 100 species in Africa, Eurasia and North America. Most of the pupfish in North America are found in springs and other suitable desert habitats in the Southwestern U.S. Other Texas pupfish include the Leon Springs Pupfish, found in the Leon Creek drainage.

Description: dark olive to bluish-gray back fading to silvery-olive sides and white belly; 5 to 8 dark gray, triangle-shaped bars on sides; spawning males develop blue coloration on back and upper sides; stout body

Similar Species: Leon Springs Pupfish (pg. 120), Red River Pupfish (pg. 120)

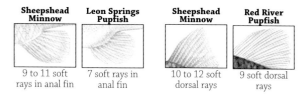

Sheepshead Minnow	Leon Springs Pupfish		Sheepshead Minnow	Red River Pupfish
9 to 11 soft rays in anal fin	7 soft rays in anal fin		10 to 12 soft dorsal rays	9 soft dorsal rays

SHEEPSHEAD MINNOW

Cyprinodon variegatus

Other Names: chubby, sheepshead killifish or pupfish, variegated minnow, broad killifish

Habitat: quiet shallows in fresh- and saltwater, such as bays, estuaries, creek, canals and ditches; tolerates low oxygen levels by gulping air at the surface

Range: Atlantic and Gulf coasts in North America, southward along the South American coast, also in the Caribbean; in Texas, native to coastal areas, introduced inland

Food: algae and other plant matter, detritus, mosquitoes, small fish

Reproduction: spawns February through October in cool waters, year-round in warmer climates; male builds pit-type nest and fiercely defends breeding territory; female deposits up to 300 adhesive eggs, which hatch in 4 to 12 days

Average Size: less than 2 inches

Records: none

Notes: A widespread little pupfish able to live in fresh- or saltwater environments, the Sheepshead Minnow also tolerates extremely low oxygen levels by gulping air at the surface. Originally found in coastal areas of Texas, it is expanding inland thanks in part to bait-bucket releases. Hybridizes with other pupfish, threatening endangered populations. Though small, it is pugnacious and will attack and kill larger fish. Used as bait by anglers, kept in aquariums and used in water pollution research.

123

Description: blue-green to brown head and back; silver lower sides, often with pink to rose stripe; sides, back, dorsal fins and tail are covered with small black spots

Similar Species: none in Texas freshwater

RAINBOW TROUT

Oncorhynchus mykiss

Other Names: steelhead, Pacific trout, silver trout, 'bow

Habitat: prefers whitewater in cool streams and coastal regions of large lakes; tolerates smaller cool, clear lakes

Range: the Pacific Ocean and coastal streams from Mexico to Alaska and northeast Russia, introduced worldwide including the Great Lakes, southern Canada and eastern U.S.; widely stocked across Texas in winter for fishing, but survives summer in few areas, only reported self-sustaining population is in McKittrick Canyon in the Guadalupe Mountains

Food: insects, small crustaceans, fish

Reproduction: predominantly spring spawners but some fall spawning varieties exist; female builds nest in well-aerated gravel in streams and lakes

Average Size: 8 to 20 inches, 3 to 8 pounds

Records: State—8 pounds, 3 ounces, Guadalupe River, 2001; North American—42 pounds, 2 ounces, Bell Island, Alaska, 1970

Notes: Several hundred thousand of these colorful trout are stocked in community fishing lakes across Texas each winter. Only able to survive summer in a few coldwater areas such as tailwaters below dams. Known for acrobatic battles and excellent table quality. Fillets are white to reddish-orange depending on diet. Caught on baits ranging from worms and salmon eggs to corn, marshmallows, artificial flies and crankbaits.

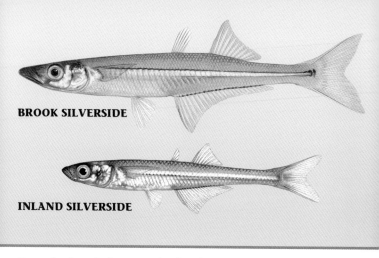

BROOK SILVERSIDE

INLAND SILVERSIDE

Description: light green back; silvery sides with bright silver stripe; long, thin body; beak-like, upturned mouth; two dorsal fins

Similar Species: Inland Silverside

Brook Silverside	Inland Silverside	Brook Silverside	Inland Silverside
beak-like jaws	lacks beak-like jaws	usually 22 to 25 anal fin rays	usually 15 to 20 anal fin rays

BROOK SILVERSIDE

Labidesthes sicculus

Other Names: needlenose or stick minnow, friar, skipjack

Habitat: surface areas of clear to slightly turbid (cloudy), warm lakes and slack-current or slow-flowing portions of large streams and rivers; uncommon in thick weed growth

Range: southeastern U.S. to the Great Lakes; in Texas, the Brazos, Red and Sabine basins

Food: aquatic and flying insects, spiders

Reproduction: spawns in late spring and early summer; males school near surface and pair with females; as the pair swims or glides downward, eggs are laid in sticky strings that attach to vegetation or the bottom; most adults die shortly after spawning

Average Size: 3 to 4 inches

Records: none

Notes: The Brook Silverside spends much of its short life (17 to 24 months maximum) cruising within a few inches of the surface, and is thought never to venture more than a few feet deep. Its flat head and upturned mouth are adaptations for topwater feeding. Most active during the day, it is often observed darting about in small schools; individuals may leap from the water in pursuit of prey or when frightened. A creature of the light, the Brook Silverside lies motionless near the surface on moonless nights, but its activity level picks up on moonlit evenings. Also attracted to artificial lights shining on the water.

127

Description: coppery, dark tan or light brown back and sides; light belly; long, flat snout with four fringed barbels on underside; long filament extends from shark-like tail

Similar Species: none

SHOVELNOSE STURGEON

Acipenseridae

Scaphirhynchus platorynchus

Other Names: hackleback, sand sturgeon, switchtail

Habitat: open, flowing channels of rivers and large streams, typically with sand or gravel bottom; tolerates turbid (cloudy) conditions

Range: Hudson Bay south through the central U.S., west to New Mexico and east to Kentucky; in Texas, the Red River below Lake Texoma

Food: aquatic insects, snails, crayfish, clams

Reproduction: spawns in spring and early summer at water temperatures of 65 to 71 degrees; adults migrate upriver or into small tributaries to spawn over gravel or rocks in swift current; will spawn below dams when necessary

Average Size: 24 inches, 3 pounds

Records: State—none; North American—8 pounds, 5 ounces, Rock River, Illinois, 2003

Notes: The smallest and southernmost of North American sturgeon species, the shovelnose has cartilage instead of bones and hard plates or scutes instead of scales. The Shovelnose Sturgeon suctions food off the bottom. Once abundant and commercially netted in some areas of its range for meat and caviar, its numbers have declined due to habitat loss.

Description: olive brown to bronze back; sides dull olive fading to white belly; blunt snout; sickle-shaped dorsal fin

Similar Species: Black Buffalo (pg. 132), Smallmouth Buffalo (pg. 134), Common Carp (pg. 68)

Bigmouth Buffalo	Black Buffalo	Smallmouth Buffalo
upper lip level with lower edge of eye	upper lip well below eye	upper lip well below eye

Bigmouth Buffalo	Common Carp
forward-facing mouth lacks barbels	downturned mouth has barbels

BIGMOUTH BUFFALO

Ictiobus cyprinellus

Other Names: baldpate, gourdhead, common or redmouth buffalo

Habitat: large lakes, sloughs and oxbows; slow-flowing streams and rivers

Range: Hudson Bay, lower Great Lakes and Mississippi River basins from Ontario to Saskatchewan south to Louisiana, widely introduced elsewhere; in Texas, the Red River below lake Texoma and the Sulphur River

Food: mostly algae and crustaceans

Reproduction: migrates to spawning shoals or flooded fields and marshes in spring when water temperatures reach the low 60s; scatters adhesive eggs over rocks, decomposing plants or debris; eggs hatch in 9 to 10 days

Average Size: 15 to 27 inches, 2 to 14 pounds

Records: State—58 pounds, 12 ounces, Sam Rayburn, 1994; North American—73 pounds, 1 ounce, Lake Koshkonong, Wisconsin, 2004

Notes: The Bigmouth Buffalo is a schooling fish typically found in the middle of the water column or near the lake bottom. Its large, forward-facing mouth and profusion of slender gill rakers are ideal for straining small food items such as crustaceans from the water. Its white, flaky meat is firm and good tasting, but it is seldom caught on hook and line.

131

Description: slate-green to dark grayish-blue back; sides gray to blue-bronze; deep body with sloping back; blunt snout

Similar Species: Bigmouth Buffalo (pg. 130), Common Carp (pg. 68), Smallmouth Buffalo (pg. 134)

Black Buffalo
upper lip well below eye

Bigmouth Buffalo
upper lip level with lower edge of eye

Black Buffalo
body width equal to distance from gill opening to snout tip

Smallmouth Buffalo
body width less than distance from gill opening to snout tip

Black Buffalo
mouth lacks barbels

Common Carp
barbels below mouth

132

BLACK BUFFALO

Ictiobus niger

Other Names: blue rooter, current or mongrel buffalo

Habitat: deep, fast water of streams and rivers; reservoirs, deep backwaters and sloughs; tolerates strong current

Range: native to the lower Great Lakes and Mississippi River basins from Michigan to South Dakota south to Louisiana, Texas, New Mexico and Mexico, introduced elsewhere; in Texas, scattered reports from the Brazos, Colorado, Red, Rio Grande and Sabine basins

Food: clams, crustaceans, algae, aquatic insects

Reproduction: spawns in spring when fish move into tributaries to deposit eggs in flooded sloughs and marshes

Average Size: 15 to 20 inches

Records: State—34 pounds, 14 ounces, Lake Texoma, 2004; North American—63 pounds, 6 ounces, Mississippi River, Iowa, 1999

Notes: The Black Buffalo is more of a bottom feeder than the Bigmouth Buffalo, it prefers deeper water more than the Smallmouth Buffalo, and it tolerates stronger currents than either one. Seldom caught on hook and line but occasionally takes doughbaits made with cottonseed meal. The firm, white meat is good table fare, particularly when smoked.

Description: slate gray or green with bronze reflections; dark eye; blunt snout; small, downturned mouth with thick lips

Similar Species: Bigmouth Buffalo (pg. 130), Black Buffalo (pg. 132), Common Carp (pg. 68)

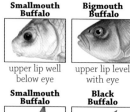

Smallmouth Buffalo

upper lip well below eye

Bigmouth Buffalo

upper lip level with eye

Smallmouth Buffalo

mouth lacks barbels

Common Carp

barbels below mouth

Smallmouth Buffalo

back steeply arched with pronounced hump

Black Buffalo

rounded back without hump

134

SMALLMOUTH BUFFALO

Ictiobus bubalus

Other Names: blue pancake, humpback or razor-backed buffalo, liner, roach back

Habitat: moderate to fast current in deep, clear streams over sand, gravel or a mixed silt bottom; less common in lakes

Range: Lake Michigan and Mississippi River basin from Pennsylvania to Montana south to Georgia, west to New Mexico into Mexico, introduced elsewhere; in Texas, found in most large streams, rivers and impoundments with the exception of the Panhandle

Food: aquatic insects, algae, clams, crustaceans, plant debris

Reproduction: spawns in spring, in slow-to-medium current, when water temperatures reach the low 60s; female deposits up to 18,000 eggs in shallow water; eggs hatch in 8 to 14 days

Average Size: 15 to 30 inches, 2 to 17 pounds

Records: State—82 pounds, 3 ounces, Lake Athens, 1993; North American—88 pounds, Lake Wylie, North Carolina, 1993

Notes: In some areas of its range the Smallmouth Buffalo is commercially harvested and a highly respected food fish. Rarely caught by recreational anglers, but a strong fighter when hooked. An opportunistic feeder, it eats plant and animal matter and is found in deeper water than the Bigmouth Buffalo and lighter current than the Black Buffalo.

135

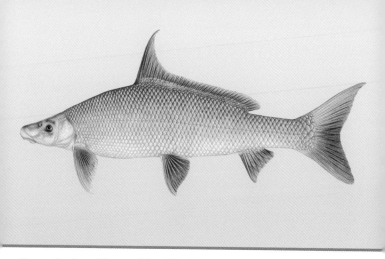

Description: blue to blue-black or olive back and upper sides fading to whitish belly; small head and long body; sickle-shaped dorsal fin

Similar Species: River Carpsucker (pg. 138)

Blue Sucker

snout longer than distance from back of eye to back of gill cover

River Carpsucker

snout shorter than distance from back of eye to back of gill cover

BLUE SUCKER

Cycleptus elongatus

Other Names: gourdseed, slenderheaded or Missouri sucker, blackhorse, schooner

Habitat: large, deep rivers and deepwater sections of reservoirs; found in moderate to fast current, often in narrow channels with rubble, sand or gravel bottom

Range: Missouri and Mississippi River drainages; found in most major stream systems in Texas

Food: insects, crustaceans, algae and other plant matter

Reproduction: typically matures at 3 to 6 years; spawns in spring at water temperatures of 50 to 60 degrees in rocky rapids; female may produce 130,000 or more adhesive eggs, which adhere to rocks

Average Size: 16 to 24 inches, 1 $^1/_2$ to 3 pounds

Records: State—none; North American—13 pounds, 3 ounces, Mississippi River, Minnesota, 1987

Notes: A migratory species, it has been negatively affected by dams, which degrade its preferred habitat by reducing current and causing increased siltation. It is reported to be the best-tasting member of the sucker family. Juveniles provide forage for game fish.

Description: brown, slate or olive back; silvery sides fading to white underside; bump in middle of lower lip; long, sickle-shaped dorsal fin; dusky dorsal fin and tail; lower fins white to pinkish-yellow

Similar Species: Blue Sucker (pg. 136), Common Carp (pg. 68)

River Carpsucker	**Blue Sucker**		**River Carpsucker**	**Common Carp**
snout shorter than distance from back of eye to back of gill cover	snout longer than distance from back of eye to back of gill cover		mouth lacks barbels	barbels below mouth

RIVER CARPSUCKER

Carpiodes carpio

Other Names: silver or white carp, quillback

Habitat: quiet, soft-bottomed backwaters, oxbows and pools of large, slow-flowing streams; seldom seen in main-channel areas; also found in reservoirs; prefers turbid (cloudy) conditions

Range: Mississippi River basin from Pennsylvania to Montana, south to Louisiana; Gulf Slope drainage from Louisiana to Texas and New Mexico; also found in Mexico; statewide in Texas

Food: aquatic insects, crustaceans, algae and other plant matter

Reproduction: matures at 2 to 3 years; spawns in late spring and summer along lake and stream shorelines; eggs are scattered randomly and hatch in 8 to 15 days with no parental care

Average Size: 15 to 19 inches, 1 1/2 to 3 pounds

Records: State—2 pounds, 1 ounce, Trinity River, 1996; North American—12 pounds, 10 ounces, Boysen Reservoir, Wyoming, 2005

Notes: Large schools of adult River Carpsuckers roam throughout reservoirs consuming massive amounts of algae. Young fish tend to favor backwater areas or rivers and streams. Juveniles may be of some importance as food for large predators, but they quickly grow too large for most other fish to eat. Large specimens occasionally reach 10 pounds in weight. Rarely caught on hook and line.

Description: golden to brassy-green back with bronze to golden-green sides and whitish belly; slate gray dorsal fin and tail; yellow-orange to dull red lower fins; blunt snout

Similar Species: Gray Redhorse (pg. 142)

dorsal and tail lack black-banded membranes

black-banded membranes on dorsal and tail

GOLDEN REDHORSE

Moxostoma erythrurum

Other Names: golden or yellow sucker, golden or smallheaded mullet

Habitat: moderately clear rivers and streams with rocky or gravel-bottomed riffles and large pools; also found in lakes

Range: Great Lake states to New England south to the Gulf of Mexico; in Texas, the Red River drainage

Food: aquatic insect larvae, mollusks

Reproduction: spawns in spring to early summer when water temperatures reach the low 60s; adults migrate into small tributary streams to deposit eggs on shallow sand or gravel bars adjacent to deep pools; no parental care

Average Size: $8^1/_4$ to 18 inches, 8 ounces to 2 pounds

Records: State—none; North American—3 pounds, 15 ounces, Root River, Minnesota, 2007

Notes: A schooling bottom-feeder with an average lifespan of 6 to 7 years, the Golden Redhorse is a hard fighter when caught on light, spinning gear. It will take live bait such as worms when fished on bottom. Excellent table fare, though somewhat bony if not prepared correctly.

Description: yellowish-gray to olive green back and sides fading to light yellow or whitish underneath; broad head with small mouth

Similar Species: Golden Redhorse (pg. 140)

Gray Redhorse	Golden Redhorse
black-banded membranes on dorsal and tail	dorsal and tail lack black-banded membranes

GRAY REDHORSE

Moxostoma congestum

Other Names: none

Habitat: rivers, streams and some impoundments; favors hard bottoms of sand or firm silt; often found in deep, slow-flowing pools and runs; tolerates moderate turbidity (cloudiness)

Range: Gulf of Mexico tributaries in Texas into Mexico and New Mexico; in Texas, the Brazos, Colorado, Guadalupe, Nueces, Rio Grande and San Antonio drainages

Food: algae, insect larvae, mollusks

Reproduction: migrates into small, clearwater creeks to spawn in March to June at water temperatures around 60 to 70 degrees; eggs are deposited over gravel or small rocks at tails of pools

Average Size: up to 25 inches

Records: State—1 pound, 3 ounces, Medina River, 2005; North American—none

Notes: Found in lakes, rivers and streams of central Texas, the Gray Redhorse is one of 100 members of the sucker family (*Catostomidae*) in North America—a dozen of which are reported in Texas. An opportunistic feeder, it has been able to adapt to some environmental changes but is still at risk from habitat loss.

Description: overall greenish coloration with horizontal rows of dark spots; large forward-facing mouth; sandpaper-like tooth patch on tongue

Similar Species: Largemouth Bass (pg. 146), Smallmouth Bass (pg. 148), Spotted Bass (pg. 150)

Guadalupe Bass	Largemouth Bass		Guadalupe Bass	Smallmouth Bass

jaw does not extend past eye

jaw extends beyond eye

tooth patch on tongue

lacks tongue tooth patch

Guadalupe Bass	Spotted Bass

coloration extends low on body

coloration doesn't extend low on body

GUADALUPE BASS

Micropterus treculii

Other Names: black bass, Guadalupe spotted bass

Habitat: streams and reservoirs but favors swift flows, particularly in streams and small rivers; common in clear spring-fed streams but tolerates moderately turbid (cloudy) conditions and temperature fluctuations; uses stumps, rocks and cypress knees as cover

Range: native to the northern and eastern Edwards Plateau, including portions of the Brazos, Colorado, Guadalupe and San Antonio rivers; introduced to the Nueces River system

Food: fish and invertebrates

Reproduction: matures at 1 year; spawns March through June with additional spawning possible through late fall; male builds nest, typically in slow-flowing pool area on firm bottom, in at least 3 feet of water; female deposits up to 9,000 eggs, which male guards after chasing female away

Average Size: less than 2 pounds

Records: State—3 pounds, 11 ounces; Lake Travis, 1983 North American—4 pounds, 10 ounces (hybrid with Smallmouth Bass), Blanco River, Texas, 1997

Notes: Found only in Texas, where it is the state fish. Because of its fondness for flowing water, it is often found in gravel riffles, flowing pools and runs. Though generally small in size, it fights hard when hooked and is fun to catch in small, free-flowing streams. Hybridizes with Spotted and Smallmouth Bass.

Description: dark green back, greenish sides often with dark lateral band; belly white to gray; large, forward-facing mouth; lower jaw extends to rear margin of eye

Similar Species: Guadalupe Bass (pg. 144), Smallmouth Bass (pg. 148), Spotted Bass (pg. 150)

Largemouth Bass	Guadalupe Bass	Smallmouth Bass	Spotted Bass
jaw extends beyond eye	jaw does not extend beyond eye	jaw does not extend beyond eye	jaw does not extend beyond eye

LARGEMOUTH BASS

Micropterus salmoides

Other Names: green bass, green trout, slough bass

Habitat: shallow, fertile, weedy lakes and river backwaters; weedy bays and weedbeds of large lakes; deep structure and flooded timber in clear, well-oxygenated reservoirs

Range: southern Canada through U.S. into Mexico, widely introduced; in Texas, found statewide except in parts of the Panhandle

Food: small fish, frogs, crayfish, insects, leeches

Reproduction: matures at 3 to 5 years; spawns March through June when water reaches 60 degrees; male builds nest on firm bottom in weedy cover; female deposits up to 40,000 eggs, which male fans and guards; eggs hatch in about 3 to 4 days; male protects fry until the "brood swarm" disperses

Average Size: 12 to 20 inches, 1 to 5 pounds

Records: State—18 pounds, 3 ounces, Lake Fork, 1992; North American—22 pounds, 4 ounces, Montgomery Lake, Georgia, 1932

Notes: The Largemouth Bass is easily the most popular freshwater game fish in Texas. It is an aggressive predator from the time it begins feeding, 5 to 8 days after hatching. Young Largemouth Bass eat tiny creatures such as copepods, water fleas and insect larvae. Before the end of the first growing season, fish are added to the menu. Two subspecies occur in Texas, the native *Micropterus salmoides salmoides* and the fast-growing Florida-strain, *Micropterus salmoides floridanus*.

147

Description: back and sides mottled green, bronze or pale gold, often with dark vertical bands; white belly; stout body; large, forward-facing mouth; red eye

Similar Species: Guadalupe Bass (pg. 144), Largemouth Bass (pg. 146), Spotted Bass (pg. 150)

no tooth patch on tongue, jaw doesn't extend past eye

Guadalupe Bass

tooth patch on tongue

Largemouth Bass

jaw extends beyond eye

Spotted Bass

tooth patch on tongue

Smallmouth Bass

vertical bars

Spotted Bass

no vertical bars

SMALLMOUTH BASS

Micropterus dolomieu

Other Names: bronzeback, brown or redeye bass, redeye, white or mountain trout

Habitat: clear, cool streams and rivers with near-permanent flow; clear lakes with gravel or rocky shores, bars and reefs

Range: extensively introduced throughout North America; stocked in numerous areas of Texas, particularly on the Edwards Plateau

Food: small fish, crayfish, insects, frogs

Reproduction: spawns March into May, when water reaches the mid to high 60s; male fans out a nest in backwaters with lake nests often next to logs or boulders; female lays up to 14,000 eggs; male guards nest and fry

Average Size: 12 to 20 inches, 1 to 4 pounds

Records: State—7 pounds, 14 ounces, Lake Meredith, 1998; North American—11 pounds, 15 ounces, Dale Hollow Lake, Tennessee, 1955

Notes: The Smallmouth Bass is a world-class game fish noted for powerful fights and wild jumps. It prefers deeper, more open water than the Largemouth Bass. In streams, it is often found over silt-free rock or gravel near riffles around rootwads and other cover—but not in the main current. In lakes, it favors riprap shores and rocky structure. Fry feed on tiny floating animals such as water fleas; at about 1.5 inches they eat small fish and insect larvae. When small-mouths reach about 3 inches long, crayfish become a pre-ferred food item and remain a staple throughout life. **149**

Description: greenish back and upper sides; rows of dark spots on whitish lower sides; distinct, sandpaper-like tooth patch on middle of tongue

Similar Species: Guadalupe Bass (pg. 144), Largemouth Bass (pg. 146), Smallmouth Bass (pg. 148)

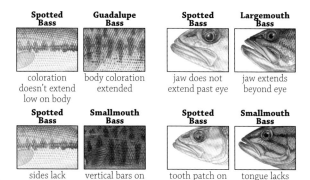

Spotted Bass	Guadalupe Bass		Spotted Bass	Largemouth Bass
coloration doesn't extend low on body	body coloration extended		jaw does not extend past eye	jaw extends beyond eye

Spotted Bass	Smallmouth Bass		Spotted Bass	Smallmouth Bass
sides lack vertical bars	vertical bars on sides		tooth patch on tongue	tongue lacks tooth patch

SPOTTED BASS

Micropterus punctulatus

Other Names: Kentucky bass, spotted black bass, spot

Habitat: warm, slightly turbid (cloudy) streams with year-round flows and main-channel areas of rivers; also found in reservoirs, often in deeper water than other bass

Range: native to south-central U.S. including East Texas, widely stocked elsewhere; in Texas, found from the Guadalupe basin to the Red River system

Food: fish, crayfish, insects

Reproduction: matures as early as 1 year old, but most spawners are 3- to 4-year-olds; male fans out nest on rock or gravel bottom at water temperatures of 57 to 74 degrees; female deposits from 1,000 to 47,000 eggs; male guards nest but moves off when eggs hatch in about 4 to 5 days, though he remains in the vicinity until fry leave the nest

Average Size: 10 to 17 inches, 10 ounces to 3 pounds

Records: State—5 pounds, 9 ounces, Lake o' the Pines, 1966; North American—10 pounds, 4 ounces, Pine Flat Lake, California, 2001

Notes: Fast-growing and prolific, the Spotted Bass coexists with other black bass but is generally found in streams that are too sluggish or warm for Smallmouths and areas with too much current for Largemouths. Despite this segregation, the arrival of Spotted Bass in some lakes led to a decline in Largemouth and Smallmouth populations, possibly due to competition for food. A popular sport fish, especially in the Cypress, Neches and Sabine systems.   **151**

Description: black to dark olive back with purple to emerald reflections; silver sides with dark green or black blotches; back slightly more arched and depression above eye less pronounced than in the White Crappie

Similar Species: White Crappie (pg. 154)

Black Crappie

usually 7 to 8 spines in dorsal fin

White Crappie

usually 5 to 6 spines in dorsal fin

Black Crappie

dorsal fin length equal to distance from dorsal to eye

White Crappie

dorsal fin shorter than distance from eye to dorsal

152

BLACK CRAPPIE
Pomoxis nigromaculatus

Other Names: papermouth, speck, speckled perch, calico bass

Habitat: quiet, clear water of streams and midsized lakes; often associated with weeds or flooded timber and brush, but may roam deep, open basins and flats

Range: native to southern Manitoba through the Atlantic and southeastern states, introduced in the West; central and eastern Texas

Food: small fish, aquatic insects, zooplankton

Reproduction: matures at 2 to 3 years; spawns in colonies in spring and early summer when water reaches the high 50s; male sweeps out a circular nest, typically over silt-free fine gravel, mud or sand; female may produce more than 180,000 eggs, which hatch in about 3 to 5 days; male guards nest and fry until young are feeding on their own

Average Size: 7 to 12 inches, 10 ounces to 1 pound

Records: State—3 pounds, 14 ounces, Lake Fork, 2003; North American—6 pounds, Westwego Canal, Louisiana, 1969

Notes: A Lone Star native, the Black Crappie is pursued year-round by anglers for its sweet-tasting, white fillets. It is an aggressive carnivore that will hit everything from live minnows to jigging spoons and small crankbaits. Adults feed heavily on other fish—shad are a main food item in some areas. Though not noted for its fighting ability, the Black Crappie puts up a good struggle on light tackle. Actively feeds at night and suspends well off the bottom in pursuit of plankton and baitfish.

153

Description: greenish to dark olive back with purple to emerald reflections; silvery-green to white sides with 7 to 9 dark, vertical bars; anal fin almost as large as dorsal

Similar Species: Black Crappie (pg. 152)

White Crappie

usually 5 to 6 spines in dorsal fin

Black Crappie

usually 7 to 8 spines in dorsal fin

White Crappie

dorsal fin shorter than distance from eye to dorsal

Black Crappie

dorsal fin length equal to distance from dorsal to eye

WHITE CRAPPIE
Pomoxis annularis

Other Names: silver, pale or ringed crappie, papermouth

Habitat: slightly silty streams and midsized lakes; more tolerant of warm, turbid (cloudy) conditions than Black Crappie

Range: native from North Dakota south and east to the Gulf and Atlantic, except peninsular Florida, widely introduced elsewhere; native to eastern Texas, now introduced statewide except in the Pecos and Rio Grande drainages

Food: aquatic insects, small fish, plankton

Reproduction: matures at 2 to 3 years; spawns on firm sand or gravel bottom in spring and early summer when water temp approaches 60 degrees; male fans out a nest, often near a log or plant roots; female deposits 3,000 to 15,000 eggs, which hatch in 3 to 5 days; male guards eggs and fry

Average Size: 6 to 12 inches, 8 ounces to 1 pound

Records: State—4 pounds, 8 ounces, Navarro Mills, 1968; North American—5 pounds, 3 ounces, Enid Dam, Mississippi, 1957

Notes: A native species, the White Crappie is popular with panfish anglers thanks to its flavorful, white fillets. It is often found in large but relatively loose schools, suspended off the bottom and away from weeds and structure. In reservoirs where flooded timber is available, however, it may be found near this woody cover. Actively feeds at night and during the winter. Due to its tolerance of turbid (cloudy) water, there is some indication of a positive relationship between the White Crappie and the Common Carp.

155

Description: dark olive to green back, blending to silver-gray, copper, orange, purple or brown on sides with 5 to 9 dark, vertical bars that fade with age; yellow underside and copper breast; dark gill spot; dark spot on rear of dorsal fin

Similar Species: Green Sunfish (pg. 158), Orangespotted Sunfish (pg. 162), Redear Sunfish (pg. 166), Warmouth (pg. 170)

Bluegill	Redear Sunfish	Bluegill	Orangespotted Sunfish
dark ear flap	orange crescent	dark ear flap	red margin on ear flap

Bluegill	Green Sunfish	Warmouth
small mouth does not extend to eye	large mouth extends to eye	jaw extends to middle of eye

BLUEGILL
Lepomis macrochirus

Other Names: bream, copperbelly, pond perch

Habitat: reservoirs and ponds, particularly those with weedy bays or shorelines; also found in oxbows of streams, and occasionally in mainstem areas below current breaks

Range: southern Canada into Mexico; statewide in Texas

Food: insects, small fish, leeches, snails, zooplankton, algae

Reproduction: typically matures by second summer; spawns from April into summer in water from 67 to 80 degrees; "parental" male excavates nest in gravel or sand, often in weeds, in colony of up to 50 other nests; smaller "cuckholder" male (exhibiting female behavior and coloration) may dart in and fertilize eggs; after spawning, parental male chases female away and guards nest until fry disperse

Average Size: 6 to 9 1/2 inches, 5 to 12 ounces

Records: State—2 pounds, .32 ounces, Lampasas River, 1999; North American—4 pounds, 12 ounces, Ketona Lake, Alabama, 1950

Notes: One of the most widely distributed panfish in North America, the Bluegill is a favorite of anglers young and old for its tenacious fighting ability and excellent table quality. Small fish are easy to catch near docks in summer. Larger "bulls" favor deeper water, often near weedlines and other cover. During the spawn, colonies are targeted and sometimes overfished. Hybridizes with other sunfish. Has acute daytime vision for feeding on small prey items, but sees poorly in low light.

157

Description: dark green back; dark olive to bluish sides; yellow or whitish belly; scales flecked with yellow, producing a brassy appearance; dark gill spot has a pale margin

Similar Species: Bluegill (pg. 156)

Green Sunfish

Bluegill

mouth extends to eye

mouth does not extend to eye

GREEN SUNFISH

Lepomis cyanellus

Other Names: black perch, blue-spotted sunfish, sand bass

Habitat: warmwater lakes with cover such as weeds or brush, or rock-rubble bottoms; also found in the backwaters of slow-moving streams and some coldwater trout fisheries

Range: most of the U.S. into Mexico excluding Florida and some areas of the Northwest; statewide in Texas

Food: aquatic and terrestrial insects, crustaceans, small fish

Reproduction: spawns in water from 60 to 80 degrees and can produce two broods per season; male fans out nest on gravel bottom in shallow water, near cover, often beneath overhanging limbs; male may grunt to lure female into nest; after spawning, male guards nest and fans eggs

Average Size: 5 to 8 inches, less than 12 ounces

Records: State—1 pound, 4 ounces, Burke-Crenshaw Lake, 2005; North American—2 pounds, 2 ounces, Stockton Lake, Missouri, 1971

Notes: The Green Sunfish is easy to catch, but not a popular sport fish because it rarely reaches more than 5 to 7 inches in length. Highly prolific, it may overpopulate a lake with stunted, 3-inch bait robbers. Tolerant of high siltation and low oxygen levels, it thrives in warm, weedy lakes and backwaters. It also withstands drought conditions and is often among the last survivors in the pools of intermittent streams. Hybridizes with Bluegill and other sunfish, producing larger, more voracious offspring.

Description: olive on blue-green back and sides with emerald or yellow speckles; head olive to orange with turquoise markings; elongated gill flap with distinct white margin

Similar Species: Bluegill (pg. 156), Dollar Sunfish, Redbreast Sunfish (pg. 164)

Longear Sunfish

white margin on gill flap

Bluegill

lacks white margin on gill flap

Redbreast Sunfish

lacks white margin on gill flap

Longear Sunfish

5 or 6 cheek scale rows

Dollar Sunfish

3 or 4 cheek scale rows

160

LONGEAR SUNFISH

Lepomis megalotis

Other Names: blackear, cherry or red-bellied bream, creek or red perch

Habitat: pools, inlets and backwater areas of clear streams with permanent flows; avoids strong current; often found near weed growth; also occurs in impoundments

Range: native to the St. Lawrence and the Great Lakes, Hudson Bay, Mississippi River and Gulf Slope drainages; west of the Appalachian Mountains from Quebec to western Minnesota south to the Florida panhandle; in Texas, statewide except Brazos and Canadian river headwaters

Food: insect larvae, fish, crustaceans, fish eggs

Reproduction: spawns late spring and early summer; male builds nest in shallow water; male courts by swimming rapidly and displaying spawning colors; female deposits eggs and male chases her away and guards fry until dispersal

Average Size: up to 6 inches and $4^{1}/_{2}$ ounces

Records: State—.48 pounds, Lake Fork, 1998; North American —1 pound, 12 ounces, Elephant Butte Lake, New Mexico, 1985

Notes: The Longear is a small but spirited and colorful sunfish, a good fighter on ultra-light gear, and a great species to introduce kids to the sport of fishing. Though small, it is good table fare. An opportunistic feeder, it sometimes darts into the nests of other sunfish or Smallmouth Bass to feed on eggs or fry if the male is distracted or taken by an angler. Similar to Dollar Sunfish of eastern Texas. **161**

Description: bluish-green back fading to orange; about 30 orange or red spots on sides of males, brown spots on females; orange pelvic and anal fins; black gill spot has light margin

Similar Species: Bluegill (pg. 156), Green Sunfish (pg. 158)

Orangespotted Sunfish

white margin on gill flap

Bluegill

lacks white margin on gill flap

Orangespotted Sunfish

hard dorsal spines higher than soft rays

Green Sunfish

hard dorsal spines shorter than soft rays

ORANGESPOTTED SUNFISH

Lepomis humilis

Other Names: orangespot, dwarf or pygmy sunfish

Habitat: ponds and lakes with open to moderately weedy areas; quiet pools and backwaters of rivers and streams

Range: Great Lakes through Mississippi River basin to Gulf States; widespread in central and eastern Texas

Food: insects, crustaceans, fish

Reproduction: matures in 2 to 3 years; spawns spring through late summer at water temperatures above the mid to high 60s; male fans out nest on coarse sand or gravel in shallow water; colonial nester; male guards nest after spawning until eggs hatch, typically in about 5 days

Average Size: 3 to 4 inches, 4 ounces

Records: State—2 ounces, Lake Fork, 2005; North American—none

Notes: A Texas native, this brightly colored little sunfish is occasionally taken by anglers but is too small to be a significant sport fish. Still, it is important as forage for other species and may help control mosquito larva in some areas. It prefers clear streams with rock bottoms but tolerates turbid (cloudy) conditions, siltation and slight pollution better than many other types of sunfish.

Description: olive to brownish back and upper sides, fading to orange or reddish belly; exceptionally long, dark gill flap

Similar Species: Longear Sunfish (pg. 160)

Redbreast Sunfish	Longear Sunfish
lacks white margin on gill flap	white margin on gill flap

Sunfish Family

Centrarchidae

REDBREAST SUNFISH
Lepomis auritus

Other Names: bream, redbelly, red throat, robin, yellowbelly sunfish

Habitat: streams, rivers and lakes; does well in a variety of habitat types, especially in slow-flowing water, where it is often found in holes near submerged rocks, timber or along overhanging banks

Range: native to the Atlantic and Gulf Slope drainages from New Brunswick to central Florida, widely introduced from Kentucky south and west to Texas; eastern and southern Texas west to Pecos drainage

Food: clams, snails, insect larvae, fish, terrestrial insects

Reproduction: matures at 2 years; spawns spring through fall at water temperatures of 60 to 80 degrees; male builds a nest on silt-free sand or gravel bottom in 1 to 3 feet of water, often along edges of pools; female deposits eggs, which are fertilized and guarded by the male

Average Size: 3 to 7 inches

Records: State—1 pound, 10 ounces, Comal River, 1997; North American—2 pounds, 1 ounce, Suwanee River, Florida, 1988

Notes: A nonnative species, the Redbreast is one of the largest sunfish in Texas. A hard fighter and fine table fare, it ranks high in popularity among Southern panfish fans. Found in clear streams of the central part of the state, especially in the San Marcos area, which is noted for healthy populations of large fish.

165

Description: bronze to dark green back and sides, fading to light green with faint vertical bars; short gill spot is tinged red on males; blue stripes on head

Similar Species: Bluegill (pg. 156)

Redear Sunfish

red crescent on gill flap

Bluegill

lacks red on gill flap

REDEAR SUNFISH

Lepomis microlophus

Other Names: shellcracker, stumpknocker, yellow bream

Habitat: prefers clear, quiet lakes with some weed growth; seldom found in current; often prefers woody cover such as submerged stumps or logs and deep bottom structure

Range: Midwest through the Southern states, introduced in the West and some northern states; native to eastern Texas, now found statewide

Food: clams, snails, insect larvae

Reproduction: matures at the end of its second year; spawns in shallow water in late spring and early summer, though in slightly deeper water than other sunfish; male builds saucer-shaped bed in gravel or silt bottom

Average Size: 8 to 11 inches, 4 ounces to 1 pound

Records: State—2 pounds, 15 ounces, Lady Bird Lake, 1997; North American—5 pounds, 12 ounces, Diversion Canal, South Carolina, 1998

Notes: Beloved by anglers for its large size and tasty white fillets, the Redear Sunfish is a southern species introduced elsewhere. It is native to much of eastern Texas but is now found statewide in suitable habitat. It rarely take baits off the surface but will hit worms and grubs, especially when fished on or near the bottom.

Description: brown to olive green back and sides with dark spots and overall bronze appearance; red eye; thicker, heavier body than other sunfish; large mouth

Similar Species: Bluegill (pg. 156), Green Sunfish (pg. 158), Warmouth (pg. 170)

Rock Bass — large mouth extends to eye

Bluegill — small mouth does not extend to eye

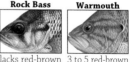

Rock Bass — lacks red-brown streaks radiating from eye

Warmouth — 3 to 5 red-brown streaks radiate from eye

Rock Bass — 6 spines in anal fin

Green Sunfish — 3 spines in anal fin

ROCK BASS

Ambloplites rupestris

Other Names: redeye, goggle eye, rock sunfish

Habitat: vegetation on firm to rocky bottom in clearwater lakes and medium-size streams

Range: southern Canada through the central and eastern U.S. to the northern edge of the Gulf States; in Texas, introduced in the Comal, upper Guadalupe and San Marcos drainages

Food: prefers crayfish, but eats aquatic insects and small fish

Reproduction: matures at 2 to 3 years; spawns in spring at water temperatures from high 60s to 70s; male fans out an 8- to 10-inch-diameter nest in 1 to 5 feet of water, on a coarse sand or gravel bottom, often next to a boulder or in weeds; male guards eggs and fry

Average Size: 8 to 11 inches, 4 ounces to 1 pound

Records: State—14 ounces, San Marcos River, 2002; North American—3 pounds, York River, Ontario, 1974

Notes: A non-native species, the chunky Rock Bass is a secretive fish that frequents weedbeds associated with rocky, sandy or gravel bottoms. It has the chameleon-like ability to change colors to match its surroundings. Though the Rock Bass is hard-fighting and good tasting, it is seldom targeted by anglers. It may feed anytime during the day, but is most active at dusk and during the night.

Description: back and sides greenish-gray to brown; lightly mottled with faint vertical bands; stout body; large mouth; red eye; 3 to 5 reddish-brown streaks radiate from eye

Similar Species: Bluegill (pg. 156), Green Sunfish (pg. 158), Rock Bass (pg. 168)

Warmouth	**Bluegill**
jaw extends to middle of eye	jaw does not extend to eye

Warmouth	**Green Sunfish**
36 to 40 lateral scales	44 to 51 lateral scales

Warmouth	**Rock Bass**
3 to 5 red-brown streaks radiate from eye	lacks red-brown streaks radiating from eye

WARMOUTH
Lepomis gulosus

Other Names: goggle eye, stumpknocker, weed bass

Habitat: natural lakes, reservoirs and slow-moving streams; prefers clear water and mud bottom

Range: southern U.S. from Texas to Florida north to the southern Great Lakes region; in Texas, statewide except the northern Panhandle streams

Food: small fish, insects, snails, crustaceans

Reproduction: spawns in spring when water temperatures reach the low 70s; not a colonial nester like other sunfish; male fans out solitary, round bed often near a rock, stump or weed clump; male guards eggs, which typically hatch in about 3 days

Average Size: 4 to 10 inches, 5 to 14 ounces

Records: State—1 pound, 4 ounces, Lady Bird Lake, 1991; North American—2 pounds, 7 ounces, Yellow River, Florida, 1985

Notes: This secretive sunfish is a solitary, aggressive sight-feeder that, when not hiding in dense vegetation, is often found around rocks and submerged stumps. It can withstand low oxygen levels, high silt loads and high temperatures. While guarding the nest, the male Warmouth drives off intruders by flaring its gills and opening its mouth, while its eyes turn blood red and its body takes on a bright yellow coloration. Its small size keeps it off the radar of many fishermen, but it has a good flavor (when taken from clean water) and is a good fighter on light tackle.

171

Description: bluish to dark olive green back; silver sides with dark, horizontal streaks; white belly; base of tongue has parallel patches of teeth; 11 to 12 soft rays in second dorsal fin; two spines on gill cover

Similar Species: Hybrid Striped Bass (pg. 174), White Bass (pg. 176), Yellow Bass (pg. 178)

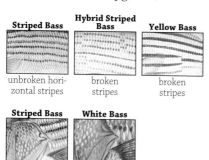

Striped Bass
unbroken horizontal stripes

Hybrid Striped Bass
broken stripes

Yellow Bass
broken stripes

Striped Bass
two spines on gill cover

White Bass
single spine on gill cover

STRIPED BASS
Morone saxatilis

Moronidae

Other Names: striper, linesides, rockfish

Habitat: fresh- or saltwater; schools roam clear water along shorelines and bays, but are also found in open water

Range: native to the East Coast of North America from lower St. Lawrence River to northern Florida and parts of the Gulf of Mexico, widely introduced from New York to the West Coast; in Texas, it is stocked in a number of reservoirs

Food: small fish (such as Threadfin Shad), insects, crustaceans

Reproduction: in water from 60 to 68 degrees, migrates into rivers and reservoir shoals in spring or early summer; successful reproduction requires constant current because the semi-buoyant eggs must remain off the bottom and have plenty of oxygen until hatching—usually in 36 to 75 hours

Average Size: 22 to 36 inches, 5 to 20 pounds

Records: State—53 pounds, Brazos River, 1999; North American—67 pounds, 1 ounce, Colorado River, Arizona, 1997

Notes: Native to the East Coast, the Striped Bass is stocked in Texas reservoirs and is the fourth most popular species among Lone Star anglers. A reproducing population exists in Lake Texoma. A schooling fish that prefers open water, it is highly adaptable, and can survive in saltwater or freshwater and water temperatures into the 90s. The Striped Bass can reach more than 100 pounds in weight but fish over 50 pounds are rare.

Description: dark gray back; bright silver sides with 7 to 8 broken stripes; dorsal fin separated, front has hard spines, rear has soft rays; two tooth patches, one on back of tongue

Similar Species: Striped Bass (pg. 172), White Bass (pg. 176), Yellow Bass (pg. 178)

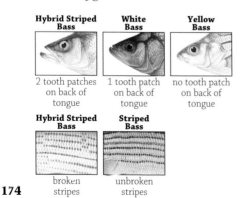

Hybrid Striped Bass

2 tooth patches on back of tongue

White Bass

1 tooth patch on back of tongue

Yellow Bass

no tooth patch on back of tongue

Hybrid Striped Bass

broken stripes

Striped Bass

unbroken stripes

HYBRID STRIPED BASS

Morone saxatilis x Morone chrysops

Other Names: palmetto or sunshine bass, whiterock, wiper

Habitat: large warmwater reservoirs and rivers with an abundant forage base

Range: no native range, a hybrid of the Striped Bass and White Bass, widely introduced from Florida and East Coast to Oregon and California; stocked in many Texas waters

Food: small fish such as shad, sunfish and silverside; also insects, crustaceans

Reproduction: generally does not reproduce successfully but makes spring spawning runs similar to parent stock

Average Size: 24 inches, 5 to 6 pounds

Records: State—19 pounds, 10 ounces, Lake Ray Hubbard, 1984; North American—27 pounds, 5 ounces, Greer's Ferry Lake, Arkansas, 1997

Notes: Texas hatcheries produce about 2.5 to 3 million hybrid stripers each year for stocking. The fish are "original cross" —the result of a male White Bass crossed with a female Striped Bass. Though smaller than purebred stripers, hybrids are able to tolerate a wider range of conditions. Also, thanks to a natural phenomenon known as "hybrid vigor," they are fast-growing, aggressive and hard-fighting.

Description: bright silver; 6 to 8 uninterrupted black stripes on each side; front hard-spined portion of dorsal fin separated from soft-rayed rear; lower jaw protrudes beyond snout

Similar Species: Hybrid Striped Bass (pg. 174), Striped Bass (pg. 172), Yellow Bass (pg. 178)

1 tooth patch on tongue

2 tooth patches on tongue

2 tooth patches on tongue

lower jaw extends past snout

lower jaw even with snout

Moronidae

WHITE BASS

Morone chrysops

Other Names: silver bass, streaker, lake bass, sand bass

Habitat: large lakes and rivers with relatively clear water

Range: Great Lakes region to the eastern seaboard, through the southeast to the Gulf, introduced elsewhere; in Texas, native to the Red River drainage, widely introduced in lakes across much of the state

Food: small fish (such as Threadfin Shad), insects, crustaceans

Reproduction: spawns in April and May at water temperatures of 55 to 79 degrees, in open water over gravel beds or rubble 6 to 10 feet deep; a single female may produce more than 500,000 eggs

Average Size: 9 to 18 inches, 8 ounces to 2 pounds

Records: State—5 pounds, 9 ounces, Colorado River, 1977; North American—6 pounds, 7 ounces, Saginaw Bay, Michigan, 1989

Notes: The White Bass is a willing striker and hard fighter that favors open water. It travels and hunts in large schools that are often spotted near the surface near dawn and dusk or in cloudy conditions. Watch for seagulls chasing frightened baitfish pushed to the surface.

Description: silvery-yellow to brassy sides with yellowish-white belly; 6 or 7 black stripes, broken above the anal fin; forked tail; two sections of dorsal connected by membrane

Similar Species: Hybrid Striped Bass (pg. 174), Striped Bass (pg. 172), White Bass (pg. 176)

Yellow Bass	**Striped Bass**	**Yellow Bass**	**White Bass**
horizontal stripes broken above anal fin	unbroken horizontal stripes	lower jaw even with snout	lower jaw protrudes beyond snout

Yellow Bass	**Hybrid Striped Bass**	**Striped Bass**	**White Bass**
lacks tooth patch toward back of tongue	two tooth patches toward back of tongue	two tooth patches toward back of tongue	one tooth patch toward back of tongue

YELLOW BASS

Morone mississippiensis

Other Names: brassy or gold bass, barfish

Habitat: open water over shallow gravel bars

Range: Mississippi River drainage from Minnesota to the Gulf of Mexico, introduced elsewhere; eastern Texas from the Red River basin to San Jacinto drainage

Food: small fish, insects, crustaceans

Reproduction: spawns in late spring, in or at the mouths of tributary streams, over gravel bars in 2 to 3 feet of water; eggs hatch in 4 to 6 days at 70 degrees

Average Size: 8 to 12 inches, 8 to 16 ounces

Records: State—2 pounds, 6 ounces, Sabine River, 2006; North American—2 pounds, 8 ounces, Tennessee River, Alabama, 2000

Notes: The Yellow Bass is similar in behavior and biology to its slightly larger cousin, the White Bass. A schooling fish, it tends to prefer more structure than the White Bass, and often is found in the middle to lower sections of the water column. In some areas of its range, the Yellow Bass is a popular panfish with anglers who consider its flaky, white fillets as superior to those of White Bass.

GLOSSARY

adipose fin a small, fleshy fin without rays, located on the midline of the fish's back between the dorsal fin and the tail

air bladder a balloon-like organ located in the gut area of a fish, used to control buoyancy—and in the respiration of some species such as gar; also called "swim bladder" or "gas bladder"

alevin a newly hatched fish that still has its yolk sac

anadromous a fish that hatches in freshwater, migrates to the ocean, then re-enters streams or rivers from the sea (or large inland body of water) to spawn

anal fin a single fin located on the bottom of the fish near the tail

annulus marks or rings on the scales, spine, vertebrae or otoliths that scientists use to determine a fish's age

anterior toward the front of a fish, opposite of posterior

bands horizontal marks running lengthwise along the side of a fish

barbel thread-like sensory structures on a fish's head often near the mouth, commonly called "whiskers;" used for taste or smell

bars vertical markings on the side of a fish

benthic organisms living in or on the bottom

brood swarm large group of young fish such as bullheads

cardiform teeth small teeth on the lips of a catfish

carnivore a fish that feeds on other fish or animals

catadromous a fish that lives in freshwater and migrates into saltwater to spawn, such as the American Eel

caudal fin tail fin

caudal peduncle the portion of the fish's body located between the anal fin and the beginning of the tail

ciénegas small, shallow wetlands in the Southwest, fed by springs or geologic formations forcing groundwater to the surface; critical habitat for some native fishes

coldwater referring to a species or environment; in fish, often a species of trout or salmon found in water that rarely exceeds 70 degrees F; also used to describe a lake or river according to average summer temperature

copepod a small (less than 2 mm) crustacean that is part of the zooplankton community

crustacean a crayfish, water flea, crab or other animal belonging to group of mostly aquatic species that have paired antennae, jointed legs and an exterior skeleton (exoskeleton); common food for many fish

dorsal relating to the top of the fish, on or near the back; opposite of the ventral, or lower, part of the fish

dorsal fin the fin or fins located along the top of a fish's back

eddy a circular water current, often created by an obstruction

epilimnion the warm, oxygen-rich upper layer of water in a thermally stratified lake

exotic a foreign species, not native to a watershed

extirpated eliminated from a geographic area, often a species' native range

fingerling a juvenile fish, generally 1 to 10 inches in length, in its first year of life

fork length the overall length of a fish from the mouth to the deepest part of the tail notch

fry recently hatched young fish that have absorbed their yolk sacs

game fish a species regulated by laws for recreational fishing

gills organs used in aquatic respiration

gill cover large bone covering the gills, also called opercle or operculum

gill raker a comblike projection from the gill arch

harvest fish that are caught and kept by sport or commercial anglers

hypolimnion bottom layer of water in a thermally stratified lake (common in summer), usually depleted of oxygen by decaying matter

ichthyologist a scientist who studies fish

invertebrates animals without backbones, such as insects, crayfish, leeches and earthworms

lateral line a series of pored scales along the side of a fish that contain organs used to detect vibrations

littoral zone the part of a lake that is less than 15 feet in depth; this important and often vulnerable area holds the majority of aquatic plants, is a primary area used by young fish, and offers essential spawning habitat for most warmwater fishes such as Walleye and Largemouth Bass

mandible lower jaw

maxillary upper jaw

milt semen of a male fish that fertilizes the female's eggs during spawning

mollusk an invertebrate with a smooth, soft body such as a clam or a snail

native an indigenous or naturally occurring species

omnivore a fish or animal that eats plants and animal matter

otolith an L-shaped bone found in the inner ear of fish

opercle bone covering the gills, also called gill cover or operculum

panfish small freshwater game fish that can be fried whole in a pan, such as crappies, perch and sunfish

pectoral fins paired fins on the side of the fish just behind the gills

pelagic fish species that live in open water, in the food-rich upper layer of water; not associated with the bottom

pelvic fins paired fins below or behind the pectoral fins on the bottom (ventral portion) of the fish

pharyngeal teeth tooth-like structures in the throat on the margins of the gill bars

pheromone a chemical scent secreted as a means of communication between members of the same species

piscivore a predatory fish that mainly eats other fish

planktivore a fish that feeds on plankton

plankton floating or weakly swimming aquatic plants and animals, including larval fish, that drift with the current; often eaten by fish; individual organisms are called plankters

plankton bloom a marked increase in the amount of plankton due to favorable conditions such as nutrients and light

range the geographic region in which a species is found

ray hard supporting part of the fin; resembles a spine but is jointed (can be raised and lowered) and is barbed; found in catfish, carp and goldfish

ray soft flexible structures supporting the fin membrane, sometimes branched

redd a nest-like depression made by a male or female fish during the spawn, often refers to nest of trout and salmon species

riparian area land adjacent to streams, rivers, lakes and other wetlands where the vegetation is influenced by the great availability of water

riprap rock or concrete used to protect a lake shore or river bank from erosion

roe fish eggs

scales small, flat plates covering the outer skin of many fish

Secchi disk a black-and-white circular disk used to measure water clarity; scientists record the average depth at which the disk disappears from sight when lowered into the water

silt small, easily disturbed bottom particles smaller than sand but larger than clay

siltation the accumulation of soil particles

spawning the process of fish reproduction; involves females laying eggs and males fertilizing them to produce young fish

spine stiff, pointed structures found along with soft rays in some fins; unlike hard rays they are not jointed

spiracle an opening on the posterior portion of the head above and behind the eye

standard length length of the fish from the mouth to the end of the vertebral column

stocking the purposeful, artificial introduction of a fish species into an area

substrate bottom composition of a lake, stream or river

subterminal mouth below the snout of the fish

swim bladder see air bladder

tailrace area immediately downstream of a dam or power plant

tapetum lucidum reflective pigment in a Walleye's eye

terminal mouth forward facing

thermocline middle layer of water in a stratified lake, typically oxygen rich, characterized by a sharp drop in water temperature; often the lowest depth at which fish can be routinely found

total length the length of the fish from the mouth to the tail compressed to its fullest length

tributary a stream that feeds into another stream, river or lake

turbid cloudy; water clouded by suspended sediments or plant matter that limits visibility and the passage of light

velocity the speed of water flowing in a stream or river

vent the opening at the end of the digestive tract

ventral the underside of the fish

vertebrate an animal with a backbone

vomerine teeth teeth on the roof of the mouth

warmwater a non-salmonid species of fish that lives in water that routinely exceeds 70 degrees F; also used to describe a lake or river according to average summer temperature

yolk the part of an egg containing food for the developing fish

zooplankton the animal component of plankton; tiny animals that float or swim weakly; common food of fry and small fish

REFERENCES

Much of the information for this book came from research presentations, the U.S. Fish and Wildlife Service and state, provincial and university departments of conservation and fisheries—most notably the Texas Parks and Wildlife Department. Other valuable sources of information on the subject include the titles listed below:

Bosanko, David. 2007
Fish of Minnesota Field Guide
Adventure Publications, Inc.

Johnson, Dan. 2007
Fish of Arizona Field Guide
Adventure Publications, Inc.

Johnson, Dan. 2007
Fish of Colorado Field Guide
Adventure Publications, Inc.

Pflieger, William. 1997
Fishes of Missouri, The
Missouri Department
of Conservation

Sternberg, Dick. 1987
*Freshwater Gamefish of
North America*
Cy DeCosse, Inc.

Thomas, Chad, Timothy Bonner
& Bobby Whiteside. 2007
Freshwater Fishes of Texas
Texas A&M University Press

Tinsley, Russell. 1988
Fishing Texas, An Angler's Guide
Shearer Publishing

INDEX

Mountain Trout, see: Chain Pickerel, Cutthroat Trout, Smallmouth Bass
Mozambique Tilapia, see: Rio Grande Cichlid
Mud Cat, see: Black Bullhead, Flathead Catfish
Mudfish, see: Bowfin
Mudminnow, see: Fathead Minnow
Mud Pickerel, see: Redfin Pickerel
Mud Shad, see: Gizzard Shad
Mullet, Striped, 100

N

Needlenose Gar, see: Longnose Gar
Needlenose Minnow, see: Brook Silverside
Northern Pike, 118

O

Orangespot, see: Orangespotted Sunfish
Orangespotted Sunfish, 162
Orangethroat Darter, 104

P

Pacific Trout, see: Rainbow Trout
Paddlefish, 102
Pale Crappie, see: White Crappie
Palmetto Bass, see: Hybrid Striped Bass
Papermouth, see: Black Crappie, White Crappie
Perch, Yellow, 112
Pickerel, see: Northern Pike, Walleye
Pickerel, Chain, 114
Pickerel, Redfin, 116
Pied Cat, see: Flathead Catfish
Pike, Northern, 118

Plains Killifish, 58
Plains Minnow, 90
Polliwog, see: Black Bullhead
Pond Perch, see: Bluegill
Pupfish, see: Red River Pupfish
Pupfish, Red River, 120
Pygmy Sunfish, see: Orangespotted Sunfish

Q

Quillback, see: River Carpsucker

R

Rainbow Trout, 124
Razor-backed Buffalo, see: Smallmouth Buffalo
Red-bellied Bream, see: Longear Sunfish
Redbelly, see: Redbreast Sunfish
Redbreast Sunfish, 164
Redear Sunfish, 166
Redeye, see: Rock Bass, Smallmouth Bass
Redeye Bass, see: Smallmouth Bass
Redfinned Pike, see: Redfin Pickerel
Redfin Pickerel, 116
Redhorse, Golden, 140
Redhorse, Gray, 142
Redmouth Buffalo, see: Bigmouth Buffalo
Red Perch, see: Longear Sunfish
Red River Pupfish, 120
Red Shiner, 96
Redside Shiner, see: Red Shiner
Red Throat, see: Redbreast Sunfish
Ringed Crappie, see: White Crappie
Ringed Perch, see: Yellow Perch
Rio Grande Cichlid, 40
Rio Grande Perch, see: Rio Grande Cichlid

ABOUT THE AUTHOR

Dan Johnson is an author and lifelong student of freshwater fish and fishing. For nearly two decades, he has brought North American anglers breaking news on the latest scientific research, fishing techniques and related technology. Dan is a longtime attendee of American Fisheries Society annual conferences and related symposia. He is editor of *Walleye In-Sider* magazine and a contributing editor to *In-Fisherman* magazine. He is the author of *Fish of Arizona* and *Fish of Colorado* field guides. Above all, he is a passionate angler who enjoys spending time on the water with his family, patterning fish behavior and observing how these fascinating creatures interact with one another in the underwater web of life. He resides in Cambridge, Minnesota, with his wife, Julie, and children Emily, Jacob and Joshua.